SHORT WALKS FROM PUBS IN

The New Forest

Anne-Marie Edwards

COUNTRYSIDE BOOKS
NEWBURY, BERKSHIRE

First published 1995
© Anne-Marie Edwards 1995

Revised and updated 1997

All rights reserved. No reproduction
permitted without the prior permission.
of the publishers:

COUNTRYSIDE BOOKS
3 Catherine Road
Newbury, Berkshire

ISBN 1 85306 345 2

Designed by Mon Mohan
Cover illustration by Colin Doggett
Photographs by Mike Edwards
Maps by Jack Street

Produced through MRM Associates Ltd., Reading
Typeset by Textype Typesetters, Cambridge
Printed by Woolnough Bookbinding Ltd., Irthlingborough

Publisher's Note

We hope that you obtain considerable enjoyment from this book; great care has been taken in its preparation. However, changes of landlord and actual closures are sadly not uncommon. Likewise, although at the time of publication all routes followed public rights of way or well-established permitted paths, diversion orders can be made and permissions withdrawn.

We cannot be held responsible for such diversion orders and any resultant inaccuracies in the text which result from these or any other changes to the routes nor any damage which might result from walkers trespassing on private property. We are anxious that all details covering the walks and the pubs are kept up to date and would therefore welcome information from readers which would be relevant to future editions.

Contents

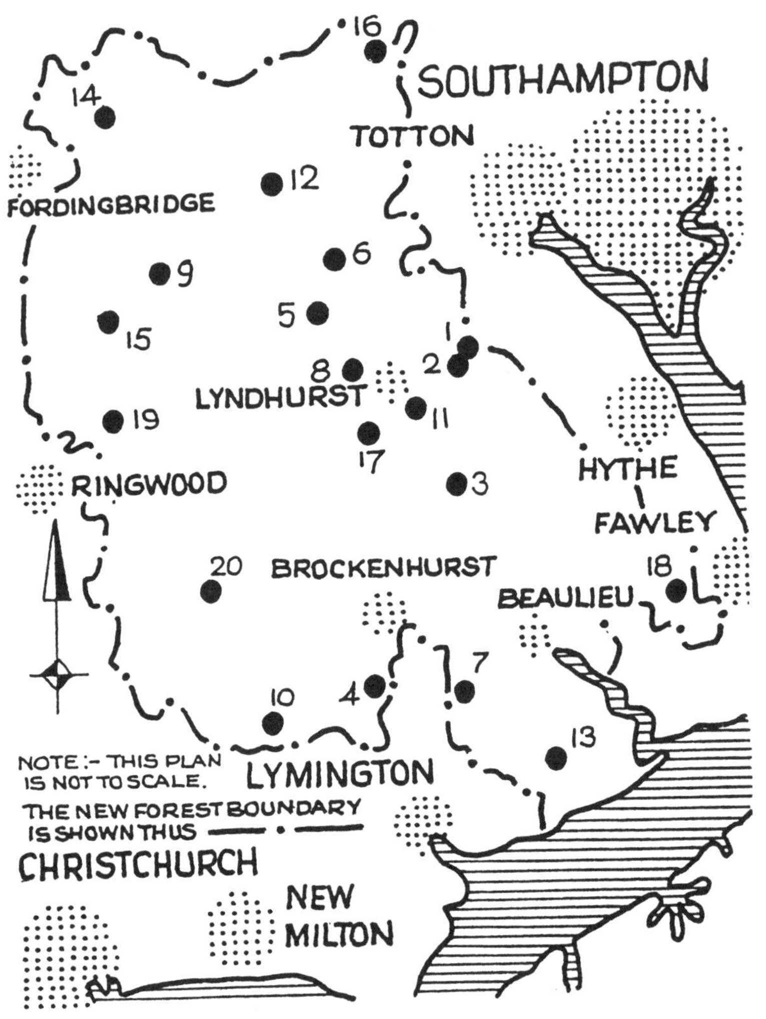

Area map showing the locations of the walks.

Introduction

To walk in the New Forest is to step back in time over 900 years. In 1079 William the Conqueror declared all the land from the Solent north to the Wiltshire Downs and from Southampton Water west to the Avon valley to be his own exclusive hunting ground. Today over 120 square miles of this 'medieval' landscape have survived, a glorious expanse of heath and woodland, still the property of the monarch though administered by the Forestry Commission. By custom this wonderful Forest, the largest medieval forest in Western Europe, is open for us all to enjoy.

The oldest woods, mainly oak and beech are termed 'ancient and ornamental' by the Forestry Commission who take care to preserve them. Many of the massive trees have been pollarded early in their growth. Without their heads, the shortened trunks sprout several branches which spread great arms over the Forest floor. As pollarding was declared illegal in 1698 when straight timber was required by the ship-building yards for England's 'wooden walls', many of these trees must be up to 400 years old. The Knightwood Oak, near Lyndhurst, has possibly stood in its sunny glade for 600 years. Oaks are home for a great wealth of wildlife and Forest rarities include the purple emperor butterfly and the lesser spotted woodpecker. Wild gladioli can be found among the bracken in the oak woods.

The famous New Forest ponies with their leggy foals are a unique breed with a wild ancestry. However appealing they may look, it is always dangerous to pet or feed them. Today they are owned by the Forest Commoners. Rights of Common in the Forest date back to Saxon times. Gradually the harsh Norman laws were relaxed and rights, usually attached to certain houses were regained. These include rights to pasture ponies, cattle, donkeys and geese and during the pannage season in autumn, when the acorns and beech seeds (mast) have fallen, the right to turn pigs out to graze . Other rights include permission to gather firewood, cut peat and spread marl dug from pits in the Forest to improve the land.

Take binoculars with you when walking these quiet ways. Herds of fallow deer, the bucks easily recognised by their wide spreading antlers, can be seen throughout the Forest. The smaller, reddish-brown roe deer have spread back from Dorset, and the little spotted sika can be seen in the southern woods. A few herds of red deer also remain in the remoter areas. The open heaths of the Forest attract many resident and migratory birds including the dainty Dartford warbler.

Although the walks in this book are short, you do not need to go far in the Forest to enjoy its peaceful seclusion. Most of the Forest is probably quieter now than at any time in its history. In the past you would have met the people who lived and worked in the Forest who depended upon it for their living. These would include gypsies, charcoal-burners, wood-cutters, snake-catchers, swineherds and even smugglers! The Forest holds their story still and what better place to tell it than at a traditional Forest pub?

All the walks are circular and start and finish at a pub serving food. The pubs have been chosen for the warm welcome they give to families and also for their authentic Forest atmosphere. All reveal differing aspects of the Forest's history, traditions and way of life. Dogs are welcome (usually on a lead and in some cases in garden areas only). All the licensees were happy for customers to leave their cars while they walked but it would be wise to ask permission first.

A note on walking in the Forest if the area is new to you. Nine hundred years of history has led to the Forest being criss-crossed by a maze of paths and there are no signposts. The sketch maps in this book are designed as guides to the starting points of the walks and they provide an overall view of the routes. So supplement them with a walker's map — I recommend the OS Outdoor Leisure Map, No 22 New Forest. The scale of 1:25 000 is ideal — about 2 $^1/_2$ inches to 1 mile. Useful aids to navigation in the Forest, which I have used several times in these walks, are inclosure boundaries. These are embankments of varying height, sometimes supporting trees or hedges, originally raised to protect areas of newly-planted trees from the animals. (They are 'inclosures' because the Forest is already an 'enclosure'). These boundaries are easy to follow and make excellent guides. However dry the weather, there is sure to be a boggy patch lurking somewhere, so wear strong shoes, boots or — like many Forest residents — wellingtons.

Finally I wish you many happy hours exploring this enchanted Forest, a source of continuing delight in all seasons.

Anne-Marie Edwards

① Ashurst
The Happy Cheese

Not long ago, two pubs, owned by a father and son, faced each other across the railway bridge at Ashurst. Father had called his the Angry Cheese so his son renamed the Monkey Puzzle Hotel on the opposite side of the road (so called because two monkey trees stood outside it) The Happy Cheese. Now only The Happy Cheese remains, providing a warm welcome to all the family at the eastern gateway to the New Forest. A wide variety of traditional English fare is on offer from 12 to 10 (9.30 on Sunday) throughout the year. Happy Cheese pies are famous, baked in a huge pie dish topped with puff pastry. You can choose between beef and ale or chicken, ham and mushroom. Daily specials include a vegetarian dish.

Drinks are served all day from 11-11 Monday to Saturday, and from 12-10.30 on Sunday. Real ales are Bass and Worthington. Cidermaster and a wide selection of wines by the glass or bottle are available.

A fully equipped playroom is provided for children and there is a pleasant garden. Dogs on leads are welcome in the garden and walkers may leave their cars in one of the pub's large car parks.
Telephone: 01703 293232

How to get there: The Happy Cheese is situated close to the row of shops in Ashurst village, just off the main A35 Southampton-Bournemouth road, on the eastern fringe of the New Forest. Driving from Southampton, turn left before the railway bridge and the pub is a few yards further on. There are trains to Ashurst (Lyndhurst Road Station) from Southampton and Bournemouth and a frequent bus service.

Parking: In one of the pub's car parks or adjacent public car park.

Length of the walk: 3 miles. Map: OS Outdoor Leisure 22 New Forest.

This easy walk following gravel tracks is suitable in dry weather for everyone including families with prams or pushchairs. As you ramble through two of the loveliest inclosures in the Forest, you may glimpse a shy roe or fallow deer deep in the peaceful oak and beech woods or, at dusk, a badger following his well-worn track. And you might like to try to solve one of the Forest's age-old mysteries as you explore historic Churchplace.

The Walk
With the front of the pub on your left, turn left along a tarmac track past the entrance to Ashurst Hospital. This large white building with its splendid view of Forest lawns and woods was originally the New Forest Union workhouse. In 1921 there were 13 officers and 110 inmates. The hospital played its part in the Second World War, caring for the wounded from Dunkirk and victims of the air raids on Portsmouth and Southampton.

The track becomes gravelled as it passes a barrier and runs alongside the village cricket ground. The woods of Churchplace Inclosure are ahead.

The track turns right through a gate into the inclosure. On the corner you pass Churchplace Cottage set in an enchanting garden. This brick cottage can have changed little since it was built in 1810 for the Keeper responsible for this area or 'Walk'. Keepers' cottages, with their orchards and paddocks, are a feature of the New Forest.

Follow the gravel track, shaded by fine oaks and beeches and bordered with wild flowers. Violets and primroses in springtime are

10

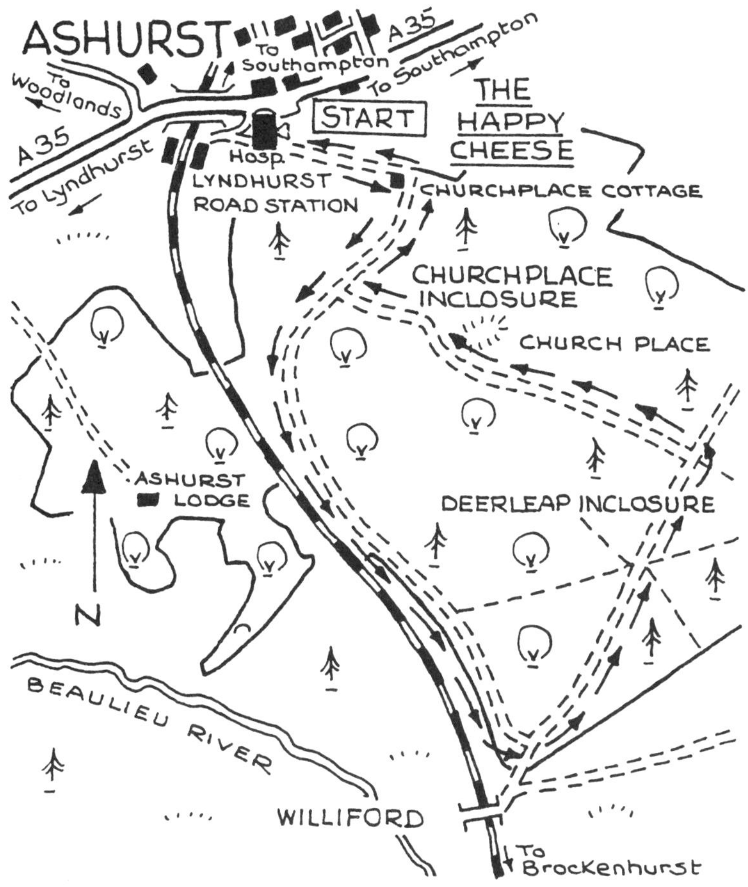

succeeded by orchids and foxgloves. Dead trees and the large Forest ant hills attract woodpeckers and all three native species can be seen here. Ignore all side tracks, keeping to the main path as it bears a little left and rises gently towards the corner of the inclosure. Our route now turns more sharply left. But I recommend you make a short detour on this corner. Leave the track to go through the gate on the right which opens onto heathland. Bear right through a scattering of trees to a bridge over the Southampton to Bournemouth railway. The line's circuitous course winding through open Forest avoiding the great woods around Lyndhurst earned it the name of Castleman's Corkscrew! A few bricks in the dell beside the line are the remains of Williford cottages, and the ford they once overlooked ran through the infant Beaulieu river. At this point the tiny stream runs almost parallel with the line and is crossed by the small bridge you see just beyond the railway.

Return to the gravel track and keep straight on over the first set of crossing tracks (there are 6 of them!) The track rises gently to meet another crossing track. Turn left here to walk through part of Deerleap Inclosure. The name commemorates a leap of 18 yards once made here by a hunted stag. This amazing feat is recorded by Gilpin in his *Remarks on Forest Scenery*. Keep on over green crosspaths, past a track on the right and a little later a green track on the left.

Our way now rises and curves a little right round some high ground dotted with tall beech trees on the right. This is Churchplace, one of several marked on New Forest maps, and possibly the site of one of the Saxon villages William the Conqueror destroyed when he claimed the region as his exclusive hunting forest. The Saxon chroniclers, who hated William, wrote that he laid waste an area of over 30 square miles and pulled down as many as 36 parish churches. Later historians have questioned this. As William Cobbett remarked when he rode through the Forest in 1832, the soil was too poor to support a large population and as 11 pre-conquest churches remained in the Forest area 'if he destroyed thirty-six parish churches, what a populous county this must have been! There must have been forty seven parish churches over the whole district — one parish church to every four and three quarter square miles'. But the name remains. The destruction of a church was sacrilege, an appalling crime for which William would certainly be doomed. Has folk memory preserved the memory of his sins for over 900 years? Leave the track to explore Churchplace with its interesting mounds and embankments and see what you think!

Continue past Churchplace down the gravel track ahead to a T-junction. Turn right along the track you followed at the start of the walk and retrace your steps, turning left past the keeper's cottage and so back to the Happy Cheese.

② Ashurst
The New Forest Hotel

This friendly Victorian pub describes itself as a family tavern and there could be no better description. It was built in 1881 as a hunting lodge to welcome Victorian visitors arriving by rail at the station close by. Among many distinguished guests was the Queen herself who probably found the same warm reception as we do today. The fame of this Forest pub has spread to the *QE2* and I was told that a party of Americans arrived one day wishing to buy one of the bathrooms which retains its Victorian fittings!

Meals are served every day from 12-2 and from 6-9.30 and there is a special menu for children. Bar snacks include some irresistible specialities. Try 'Smokey Joes'(hickory smoked chicken wings) or one of the wide range of deep pan pizzas which include a vegetarian and a sea food dish. Drinks are served all day from 11-11 in summer, Monday to Saturday. In winter the hours are from 11-2.30 and 6-11. On Sunday normal pub hours apply. There are always three traditional ales available, Tetleys and two others, possibly Wadworth 6X and Salisbury Brewery's Summer Lightning. Old English and Gaymers cider and a full range of wines are served. There is a no-smoking area in the restaurant.

Children are specially welcome inside where there is plenty of room away from the bar areas. While parents relax over a drink in the garden, which overlooks the open Forest, children can enjoy themselves in a playground and watch the donkeys, sheep and hens. Dogs should be kept on leads.

The pub also offers accommodation and is perfectly placed for an enjoyable family holiday in the New Forest.

Telephone 01703 292319 for details.

How to get there: The entrance to the New Forest Hotel faces the small station at Ashurst (Lyndhurst Road Station). Approaching from Southampton along the A35, pass the row of shops in Ashurst village, cross the railway bridge, then after a few yards turn left for the station. The pub is on your right.

Parking: In the pub's car parks or, if there is no room, Ashurst public car park. This is on the other side of the railway. Return across the bridge and turn immediately right, then right again, past the Happy Cheese pub. Cross the entrance to Ashurst hospital to the public car park which is on your left.

Length of the walk: 3 ¹/₂ miles. Map: OS Outdoor Leisure 22 New Forest.

The old oak and beech woods of the New Forest, known as 'ancient and ornamental' are famous for their beauty and this easy walk includes a ramble in one of the finest at Matley. This glorious oak wood is home to many wild creatures, including deer and badgers. To reach Matley we follow narrow tracks over wide heaths and green lawns cropped short by the semi-wild ponies, to enjoy the ever-changing contrasts of scenery which add so much to the charm of the New Forest.

The Walk

If you have visited the pub, you can start this walk from the pub garden. With your back to the pub, walk over the lawn past the children's playground and cross the stile ahead to open grassland. There is no path at this point but walk straight ahead with Ashurst

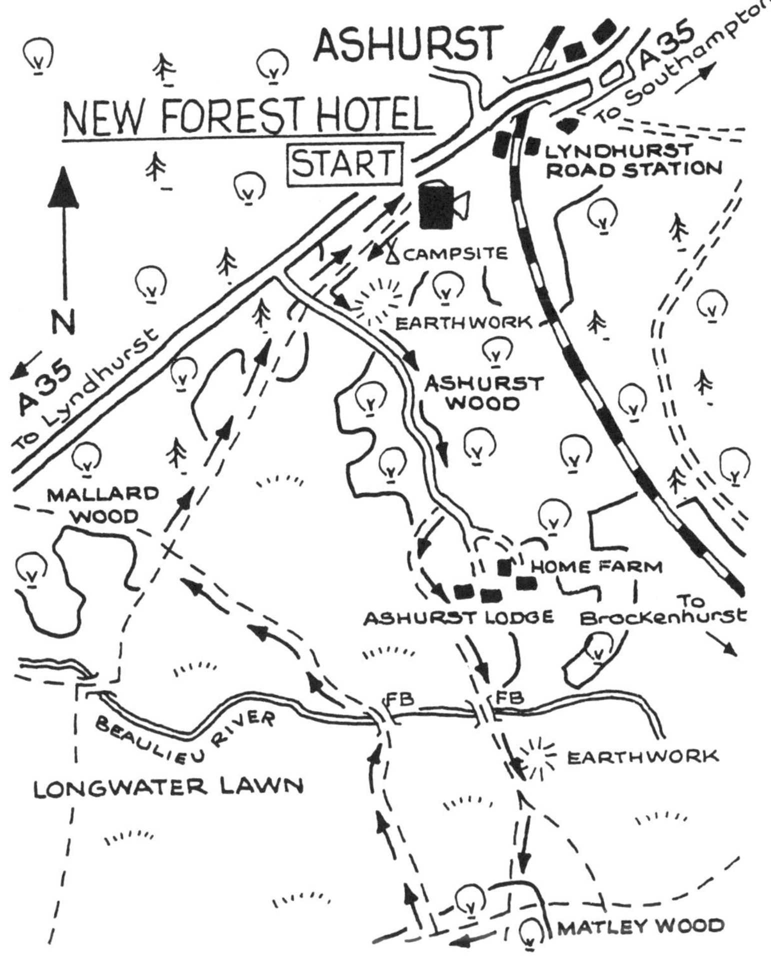

campsite on your left and the A35 on your right. Otherwise, walk up to the A35, turn left beside the road for a few yards, then cross a small stile leading to the grassland on your left. Keep ahead until you are level with the New Forest Hotel garden, then bear right to follow the directions above. Cross the road to the campsite and keep straight on parallel with the A35 which is about 150 yards away on your right. Woods soon hide it from view, and in a small wood on your left you will see the embankments of an earthwork, possibly an Iron Age farm.

Fallow deer

In a little under a quarter of a mile you reach the road leading from the A35 to Ashurst Farm and Ashurst Lodge. Turn left and follow the road until you see the Lodge and entrance to the farm directly ahead. Leave the road and turn right past a Forestry Commission barrier, over a parking area. A clear path bears left close to the Lodge fence, and peaceful Forest scenes now surround you. From the path, heaths, dotted with small woods slope down to a shallow valley, giving beautiful views over the Forest as far as Lyndhurst. The spire of the church rises on the skyline. Follow the path, keeping the fence on the left. The path dips to a bridge over Longwater stream, one of many small waterways that thread this heathland on their way to meet the Beaulieu river. These tiny streams, stained by iron the colour of old sherry, are blanketed in spring with white crowfoot .

Follow the path as it rises gently up the heath ahead past some more interesting embankments on the left which I feel could be another Iron Age site. At the highest point the path forks. Take the right-hand fork to make your way to the outlying birches, yews and pines that form the approach to the great oak wood at Matley. An inviting grassy path leads you into the wood. Just after entering the wood, the path divides. Bear right keeping the edge of the wood

16

about 50 yards away on your right. Many of the great oak trees were cropped or pollarded before the practice was declared illegal in 1698, and without their heads, the main trunks have sprouted several stems, which now spread massive arms far over the Forest floor. Wild flowers flourish in the dappled sunlight beneath them, and the host of insect life they attract brings a wide variety of woodland birds including the rare lesser spotted woodpecker. The drumming of woodpeckers against the oak trees and their harsh calls or 'laughter' echo through the summer woods. The deer you are most likely to see here, and grazing on the surrounding heathland, are fallow with their wide spreading antlers and distinctive white rump and the smaller, reddish-brown roe with their small upright antlers and graceful movements. Fallow deer gather in herds and in the rutting season, around October and November, the buck will stand guard over his hinds defying all challengers. Roe prefer to live in small family groups and will often be seen with their fawns.

Continue along the edge of Matley Wood until you leave the trees and meet a crosspath. Turn right so that the wood is now behind you and keep straight on over the open lawn ahead following the path which runs to the left of a line of gorse bushes. This leads to open heath where the path bears slightly left towards a band of woodland. The path curves a little right to meet a bridge over the Longwater. From the bridge, keep straight ahead over the lawns to the heath and continue ahead towards the woodland. Cross a junction of several narrow paths. Just past them the path divides. Follow the left-hand path which bears slightly left, still heading for the woods. When you reach the wood, keep ahead through the fringing trees to meet a good crosstrack. Turn right and follow this track as it traces the edge of the wood and crosses small heaths. It disappears under fallen leaves and trees at times but just keep straight ahead. You will hear traffic sounds from the A35 on your left and soon see Ashurst campsite on your right. Dotted among younger trees are some magnificent ancient oaks, their creased and creviced branches supporting gardens of ferns. Cross the road to Ashurst Lodge and walk over the heath to the New Forest Hotel which you will see directly ahead.

③ Beaulieu Road
The Beaulieu Road Pub

Long, low and welcoming this ideal family pub is built around a courtyard in the heart of the Forest. The Inn is spacious and the restaurant offers accommodation for 90 people. A large garden, with a playground for children (including a Wendy house) overlooks the open heath and ancient oak woods. The pub is a hive of activity and crowded with colourful Forest characters during the Beaulieu Road pony sales which are held close by, six times a year from August to December and also in April. If you would like to join in the fun, ring the pub for details.

Visitors should have hearty appetites to appreciate the home cooking which includes steak and kidney pies, lasagne, a vegetarian dish, and old-fashioned sweets such as apple crumble and treacle pudding. Meals are served lunchtimes 12-2.30 and evenings 6-9 (9.30 on Saturdays). On Saturday and Sunday the pub serves drinks from 11 in the morning to 11 at night. On other days drinking hours are from 11-3 and 6-11. Dogs are welcome in the bar area where they have a special corner set apart for them!

Traditional ales are Wadworth 6X and the locally brewed Ringwood Old Thumper. Dry Blackthorn cider is available and a wide range of French and German wines. If you bring sandwiches for your walk, no one objects if you eat them in the garden providing you buy a drink.

Telephone: 01703 292342

How to get there: The pub stands beside the B3056 at the point where the road crosses the main Southampton—Bournemouth railway. Approaching along the A35 from Southampton, turn left along the Beaulieu road, B3056, just before you enter Lyndhurst. Follow the road for about 4 miles, cross the railway bridge and the pub is immediately on your right.

Parking: Either in front of the pub or in the pub car park. To reach the park, drive past the pub and the Beaulieu Road Hotel which is adjacent, then turn right to the pub car park which is behind the hotel parking area.

Length of the walk: 3 ¹/₂ miles. Map: OS Outdoor Leisure 22 New Forest.

This fascinating walk in a remote area in the heart of the Forest is a favourite with bird watchers. The wide heaths around the pub are home to a Forest rarity — Dartford warblers. More exotic migratory birds such as golden orioles may also be seen there. Denny Wood, classed as 'ancient and ornamental' is one of the last refuges of the lesser spotted woodpecker. The famous Beaulieu Road pony sales are held close by and there is a Forest mystery to solve as you walk.

The Walk

Walk back to the road from the car park, and with the front of the pub on your left, continue beside the road over the railway bridge. The wooden pens on the right are the setting for the pony sales. It is an exciting spectacle. Although New Forest ponies are owned and cared for by the Commoners, whose right to pasture animals dates back to Saxon times, the ponies are wild and allowed to roam freely. When they are rounded up for marking or sale, they remember their wild ancestry and head for cover. The resulting scenes are reminiscent

In Denny Wood

of the Wild West! When broken, the ponies make excellent mounts but when loose on the Forest they can be dangerous particularly at foaling time, so it is wise to keep your distance and not to feed them.

Follow the road for a few yards to the gravel track leading left to Shatterford Bottom car park within its sheltering grove of scented pines. Turn left and follow the track to the car park, then bear a little left over the parking area, past a Forestry Commission barrier to continue along a wide path over the heath. Apart from a glimpse of a dainty Dartford warbler, you may see other nesting birds including curlews, lapwings, nightjars, redshanks and woodlarks.

Small bridges lead over marshy areas scented with bog myrtle, known locally as gold-withey. The berries of this small shrub were once used to flavour gin. The path climbs a little then divides. The left-hand path leads to a bridge over the railway, but our way is right towards Denny Wood. The heath becomes dotted with small pines and the path cuts across the long line of an earth embankment. This forms part of the boundary of Bishop's Dyke, a marshy expanse about a mile in length and half a mile wide, which, until quite recently belonged to the Bishop of Winchester. John de Pontisarra, Bishop of Winchester, persuaded Edward I to allow him to enclose

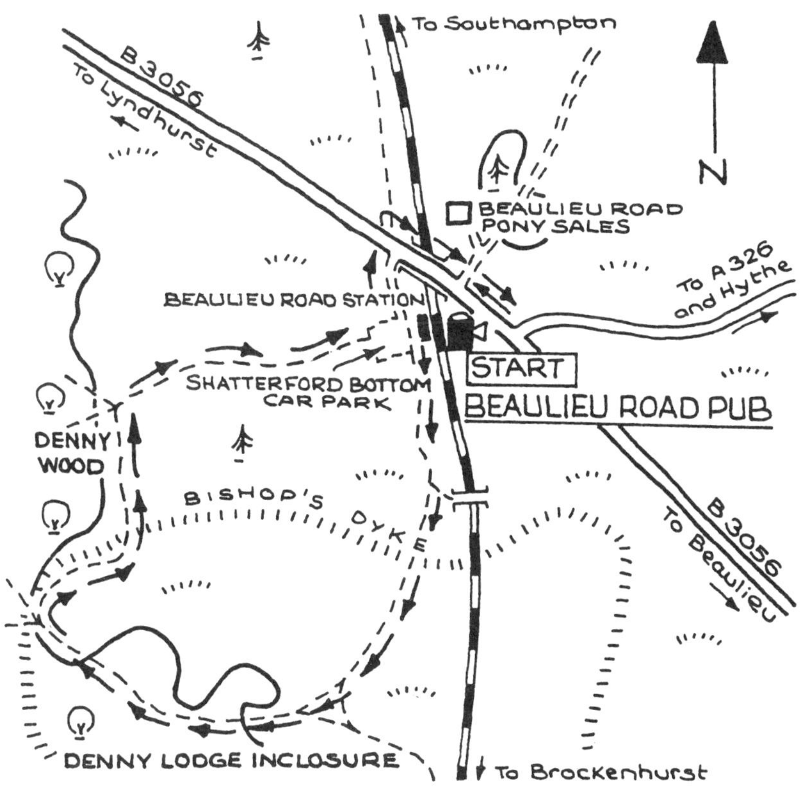

the land in 1284. And here is another New Forest mystery! Why should a medieval Bishop want this marsh? Was he a keen wildfowler eager to claim the best snipe shooting in the area? Or was the land drier then and he only wanted pasture for his ponies? Naturally, Forest legend tells a more dramatic tale. In ancient times, it is said, a Winchester prelate was promised as much New Forest land as he could crawl round in twenty-four hours. The wavering course of the boundary certainly does suggest the route of someone in difficulties!

The path leads through the pine-dotted heath and curves a little right as it approaches the birches fringing the oak woods of Denny. Cross two small bridges and just after the second the path becomes indistinct in front of a grove of birches. Bear a little right round the grove to resume your former heading along a clear path. On either side stand some of the mighty giants of the Forest, massive oaks over

21

500 years old. Cross a small heath and you will see a gate ahead. About 50 yards before the gate, our path meets a crosstrack. Turn right to follow a beautiful path over the heath occasionally shaded by the great trees of Denny Wood. Follow the path as it crosses two small bridges. The fence enclosing the woodland is on your left. Cross a small heath and keep on over another small bridge. The path now bears right to take you across two more bridges. Just after the second bridge you need some careful navigation for a few yards. Ignore the little path that runs along the bank of the stream on the right, but bear half-right for about 50 yards, leaving the denser wooded area on your left. You will see an embankment (more of Bishop's Dyke) on your left. Keeping the embankment about 30 yards on your left, continue along the fringe of the wood along a path which soon becomes well defined. Keep to this main path as it curves slightly left beside the wood. After about a quarter of a mile, the path turns left uphill. From the top of the slope there are wide views over woods and heath towards the Beaulieu river. The path winds through groves of silver birches and over small heaths to meet a crosstrack in a more open grassy area. Turn right to follow the path over the heath towards Beaulieu Road. The row of whitewashed cottages beside Beaulieu Road station form a landmark ahead, a little to the right of the path. The pines of Shatterford car park soon come into sight beside the path. Cross the car park, follow the gravel track to the road, and turn right to retrace your steps to the pub.

④ Setley
The Filly Inn

This old world hostelry offers a warm welcome to all the family. Although it is situated beside a busy main road, once inside you will enjoy a real New Forest atmosphere. Close by stands the Marlpit Oak where highwaymen once demanded your money or your life. And to remind us of those days the ghost of a repentant highwayman now haunts the pub. I was told he is a friendly old gentleman who plods around at quiet times! The long straight road outside the pub was constructed to make the way easier for teams of horses to drag the huge New Forest oaks to Lymington to build ships for Nelson's navy.

All the food is home-cooked and includes steak and mushroom pie and delicious New Forest country sausages. Fresh fish is also available. During the summer (and winter weekends) the Filly is open all day. At other times the hours are from 11-2.30 and from 5-11.

Real ales are Ringwood Old Thumper, and Best Bitter and Bass and various guest beers from local breweries. Provided visitors purchase food or drinks, they are welcome to use the car park. Dogs have a drink provided for them in the garden. The Inn caters for private parties and offers bed and breakfast accommodation.
Telephone: 01590 623449

How to get there: The pub is situated beside the A337, about a mile south of Brockenhurst. From Lyndhurst, take the A337 Lymington road. Drive through Brockenhurst village, cross the railway and continue past Holly Bush nurseries and vineyard. The Filly Inn stands to the left of the road about a quarter of a mile past the nurseries.

Parking: In the pub car park.

Length of walk: 3 ½ miles. Map: Outdoor Leisure 22 New Forest.

Most of this walk is through an SSSI, Roydon Woods nature reserve. These beautiful mixed woodlands are ungrazed and shelter a wealth of wildlife. There is a fine view of Roydon Manor where W.H.Hudson wrote 'Hampshire Days' and an unforgettable glimpse of the upper reaches of the Lymington river.

The Walk

We start from the pub car park. With your back to the main road and the side of the pub on your left, cross the car park and turn left through a small iron gate. Descend the steps and turn right along a narrow lane. This was once the main road to Lymington!

After a few yards, turn left over a cattle grid along a track signed 'Private, Bridleway only'. A pretty tree-shaded way leads you beside a green valley to enter the woods of Roydon nature reserve. The reserve comprises 750 acres of the Lymington river valley and is mainly broadleaved woodland. Come here in May to see the blue-bells! Other wild flowers include the blue and pink flowered lungwort. Among the wealth of butterflies is another of the Forest's treasures, the Silver Washed Fritillary. Foxes and badgers are common. The woods are also home to all four species of Forest deer — red, fallow, roe and sika.

The track through the woods passes some deep pits which you will see throughout the New Forest. These were dug for 'marl' which was an ancient method of fertilising poor land by spreading over it material dug from more fertile areas. The 'right of marl' is still possessed by some Commoners. When you come to a crossing track by footpath signs, turn right. The track dips downhill and passes the private entrance to Roydon Manor. Keep on until you see a footpath sign on the right indicating a right-of-way on the left. Turn left

24

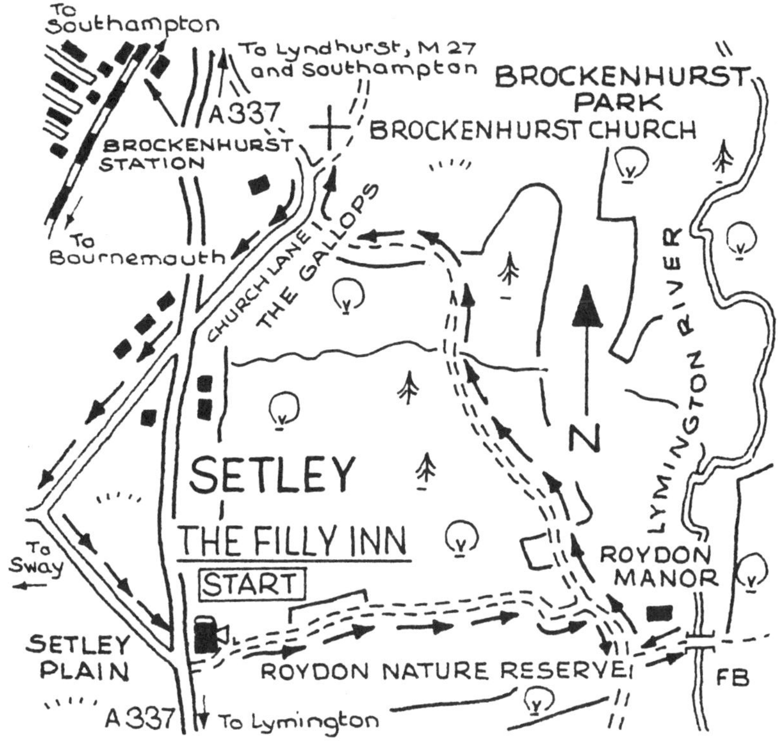

through two gates along a path bordered by flower-filled meadows. After about one hundred yards look left for a splendid view of Roydon Manor, a gracious seventeenth century house. W.H.Hudson, the author of *Hampshire Days* came to live here at the turn of this century. The house still looks very much as he describes it: 'an old picturesque red-brick house with high-pitched roof and tall chimneys, a great part of it overrun with ivy and creepers, the walls and roof stained by time and many-coloured lichen to a richly variegated greyish red.' Passionately interested in wildlife he spent most of his time minutely observing the birds and insects in the New Forest. Small insects fascinated him. Observing that female grasshoppers were often ignored by the males and would sit patiently alone for hours, he carried one into the house on a wild rose branch. After she had eaten all the berries on her branch he kept her alive for sixteen days on a diet which included bread pudding and ginger beer!

The naturalist did not have far to go to enjoy one of the Forest's most enchanting scenes. Follow in his footsteps past the house to where the path drops to cross the Lymington river by a small wooden footbridge. The water flows swiftly beneath the boughs of overhanging willows and round the spreading roots of massive oaks. Tall stands of irises fringe the banks and woodland flowers tuck themselves into every hollow. This is a place to 'stand and stare'.

From the bridge retrace your steps past Roydon Manor, turning right at the crosstrack to return to the footpath signs at the top of the rise. To continue the walk, keep straight on along the track ahead through another beautiful part of the nature reserve.

The way winds uphill to more open countryside and on the right you will see the parkland which once surrounded Brockenhurst Manor, the home of the Morant family. The manor has gone, but the fine park planted with some glorious cedars remains. The path crosses a wide grassy avenue known as 'The Gallops'. This was the training ground of 'Lovely Cottage' a Grand National winner.

When the path reaches a minor road, Church Lane, you can if you wish make a short detour to visit Brockenhurst Church. To do so, turn right and you will see the church ahead after less than a quarter of a mile. It is the oldest church in the Forest, incorporating Saxon herring-bone masonry. An enormous yew, which, like the church is mentioned in the Domesday Book, stands to the left of the south porch. Among many fascinating features inside the church is a curtained, boxed-in 'Squire's pew'. Walk down the hill to the east side of the churchyard to see the beautifully kept memorial to the New Zealand and Indian soldiers who lie there. Brockenhurst village played its part in both world wars; during the first it was the home of a base hospital. Close by is the grave of 'Brusher' Mills, a well-known nineteenth century snake-catcher. His headstone shows him holding a handful of lively-looking snakes outside his Forest home, a simple wigwam of branches covered with turf. To continue the walk, retrace your steps and continue down Church Lane.

If you do not visit the church, turn left when the path meets the lane and walk down to the main road, A337. Cross straight over and follow the lane ahead to meet a minor road. Turn left to walk over the open Forest heath, parallel with the minor road to cross the cattle grid before the main road, A337. Turn left and walk over the road to the Filly Inn.

5 Minstead
The Trusty Servant

Once you have discovered this friendly pub facing the village green in Minstead it will become a favourite with all the family. There can be few better ways to spend a summer evening than to sit outside with a drink and share the festivities — still an important part of life in this charming old world village. These include Morris dancing and celebrations at Whitsun and Easter, when the Forest Mummers' plays are revived. The unusual inn sign also recalls the past. This depicts 'the trusty servant' who turns out to be a pig with a padlocked snout to illustrate his discretion and stag's feet to indicate his speed in running errands. He is armed with sword and shield to protect himself and his master. It is copied from a picture in Winchester College.

But the food is very much up to date! Meals are served all week from 12-2 and 7-10 (9.30 on Sunday). Apart from the regular menu — try Murphy's Pie — there is a splendid range of fresh sea food including blue marlin, swordfish and red snapper. I recommend trying the chowder and moules. Drinking hours are from 11-11

Monday-Saturday in the summer, from 11-3 and 6-11 in winter. Normal hours are observed on Sunday. Real ales are Wadworth 6X, Flowers Original, Ringwood Ales and Boddingtons. Draught cider and a wide range of wines are available. Dogs on leads are welcome. The pub offers accommodation. Tel: 01703 812137 for details.

How to get there: The pub is in the centre of Minstead, a small village just to the north of Lyndhurst surrounded by a network of minor roads between the A31 and A35. From Lyndhurst take the Romsey road (A337) and after about 1 ½ miles turn left following the directions for Minstead. Approaching from Southampton follow the road to the Cadnam roundabout, then take the A31 turning left for Minstead after about 2 miles.

Parking: There is a small pub car park but if this is full you can use the parking area on the other side of the road. If all else fails, drive up the lane to the church (the front of the pub is on your right) and park under the trees beside the churchyard.

Length of the walk: 2 miles. Map: OS Outdoor Leisure 22 New Forest.

This is a Forest walk with a difference! The gentle pastoral countryside around Minstead is more reminiscent of a lush Hampshire river valley than an ancient hunting Forest. But here the views are always framed by beautiful Forest woods and great oaks shade the field paths. The walk includes a visit to Furzey Gardens, at its loveliest in the spring.

The Walk

Leave the pub on your right and with the village green on your left follow the narrow lane signposted *To the Church*. The little church stands on top of the hill and is one of the most fascinating in the Forest. It has a comfortable cottage-like appearance and is built of traditional Forest materials, wattle and daub — stone could only be spared for the arches and corners of the main walls. The church has an old gallery and a rare three-decker pulpit. The sermon was preached from the top level, the Scriptures were read from the second, while the parish clerk with just an 'Amen' to say occasionally had to be content with the lowest level. In the churchyard you

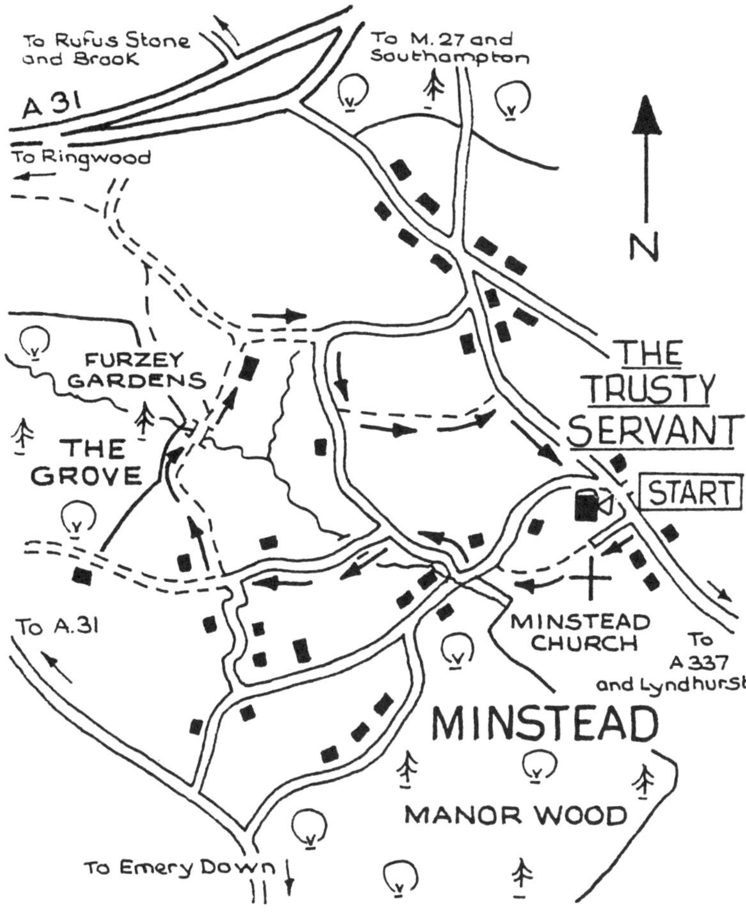

will find a stone cross marking the grave of Sir Arthur Conan Doyle who lived at Bignell Wood close by. He wrote about Minstead in *The White Company*.

From the church, follow the footpath that runs from the road to the right of the churchyard. A pleasant green valley lies ahead leading to Manor Wood. The path bears a little right to enter this mixed wood of oaks, beeches, silver birches, rowans and holly. Leave the wood through a gate and turn right to meet a minor road. On your left a small Forest stream cuts its way under the tree roots through green lawns. Across the road, a little to your left, you will see

Minstead's delightful church has the look of a cottage

a sign for Furzey Gardens. Follow the sign up the lane past the old school. The lane rises to a road junction on the left by a small grassy triangle. Turn left to take this narrow, leafy lane as it drops to ford a stream. Cross the bridge and keep on up the hill past some old world houses and farms.

When the lane turns sharply left, you will see two footpaths, one leading straight on and the other leading over a stile on the right. Turn right, over the stile and follow the very narrow footpath ahead which soon drops downhill to a stream. Bear left over the bridge, climb the stile and walk up the meadow ahead to another stile. When you have climbed this one, turn immediately right (yellow arrow footpath signs point the way). A woodland path leads down to a stream. Cross the bridge and climb the wooden walkway ahead to continue up the slope through glorious oak and beech woods with a small stream purling over the stones on your right. When the path divides take the right-hand path so that the stream is still on your right. Cross a bridge over the stream which now is on your left and continue uphill to a fenced section. Just beyond, the path divides again. Take the left-hand path and now the scent of flowers hints at the beautiful garden waiting to be visited. The path winds up to a

30

wider track which runs to the left of Furzey Gardens. The entrance is on your right.

Furzey is not a large garden. The massed banks of flowering shrubs and trees intersected by tiny paths leading to small pools and pergolas, colour a gently sloping hillside which merges almost imperceptibly into the surrounding meadows and woodlands. It is a true Forest garden with magnificent azaleas and rhododendrons which flourish on the acid soil. One very rare azalea is said to have been brought from the garden of the Emperor of Japan. There is a woodland area with tree houses for children to scramble about in.

If you would like to find out more about the everyday lives of Forest workers in the past there is a perfect opportunity at Furzey. A 400-year-old cottage has been carefully preserved at the entrance and the kitchen, with its enormous open fireplace filled with an assortment of 16th and 17th century cooking utensils is unchanged. To one side is the circular bread oven and behind the oven, part of the wattle and daub of the cottage walls is visible. Old ships' timbers from Tudor shipyards at Lymington form the roof beams and upstairs flooring. Upstairs there are only two tiny bedrooms and yet the cottage once housed a family with 14 children! The last of the children died in 1942. By the cottage a large gallery displays a wide variety of local arts and crafts.

Leave the entrance to the garden on your right and continue down the track to meet a lane. Turn right down the lane and when it divides in front of a grassy area turn right again. After a few yards, turn right once more. Continue along the lane for about 150 yards, then look for a stile by a footpath sign on your left. Turn left over the stile and follow the field path with a hedge on your left. Cross the next stile and climb the field ahead to another stile which leads to a lane. Turn right along the lane and after a few yards bear left through a gap in the hedge in front of a gate to continue along a little footpath parallel with the road. This quickly brings you back to the Trusty Servant pub.

6 **Canterton Glen**
The Sir Walter Tyrrell

As you would expect, a Forest that has survived for over 900 years must have its share of mysteries. Close to the Sir Walter Tyrrell pub in Canterton Glen a who-dun-it took place that has baffled historians for centuries. On the second day of August, in the year 1100, William II, surnamed Rufus, was shot dead by an arrow from the bow of Walter Tyrrell. But did Sir Walter really fire the fatal arrow? The inn is named after the supposed assassin. You can also visit the Rufus Stone which marks the spot where the King fell, to look for clues!

There are plenty of other good reasons to visit this beautifully sited pub. I was impressed with the warm welcome and the care that the management takes of its younger guests. Children have a well-equipped and supervised playground, their own tuck shop and separate facilities. Meals are served all day in July and August and at other times from 12-2.15 and from 6-9.30. Among many delicious dishes try the rack of lamb, steak-and-ale pie, mussels, a mega mixed grill or one of the very reasonably priced steak promotions. There is a vegetarian menu and a choice of 'light bites'.

Children have their own special menu. Drinks are served all day from 11-11 in July and August and also all day on Saturdays and Sundays throughout the year. For the rest of the year, drinking times are from 11.30-2.30 and 7-11. Real ales include Bass, Ruddles County, John Smith's Smooth, No Name Bitter and Courage Directors. Craft fairs are held at weekends in July and August. Dogs are welcome in the garden which is separate from the children's play area. The pub car park does get very crowded at peak times, but the landlord is happy for walkers to leave their cars provided they enquire first.
    Tel: 01703 813170.

How to get there: Approaching from the east along the M27 continue past the junction with the A31 for about 1 ½ miles. Turn right across the central reservation as directed for the Rufus Stone. Turn right along the eastbound carriageway for a few yards then left down the minor road signposted for the Rufus Stone. Drive past the stone to the pub which is on your right. From Lyndhurst, take the A337 for Romsey, turn left to join the A31 at the Cadnam roundabout to continue to the right turn across the central reservation for the Rufus Stone.

Parking: In the pub car park. If the pub car park is busy, there is a large public car park opposite the Rufus Stone a few yards up the lane in the direction of the main road.

Length of the walk: 2 miles. Map: OS Outdoor Leisure 22 New Forest.

This is an easy stroll through Forest glades that can have changed little since they witnessed the death of William Rufus. As well as a visit to the Stone where tradition records he fell from his horse with an arrow through his heart, the ramble explores a remote Forest hamlet whose first settlers probably arrived long before William the Conqueror.

The Walk
With the front of the pub on your left, walk back up the lane towards the main A31. After a few yards you will come to a car park on the left and see the grey oblong of the Rufus Stone across the grass opposite. The Saxon chroniclers, who tell the story of what hap-

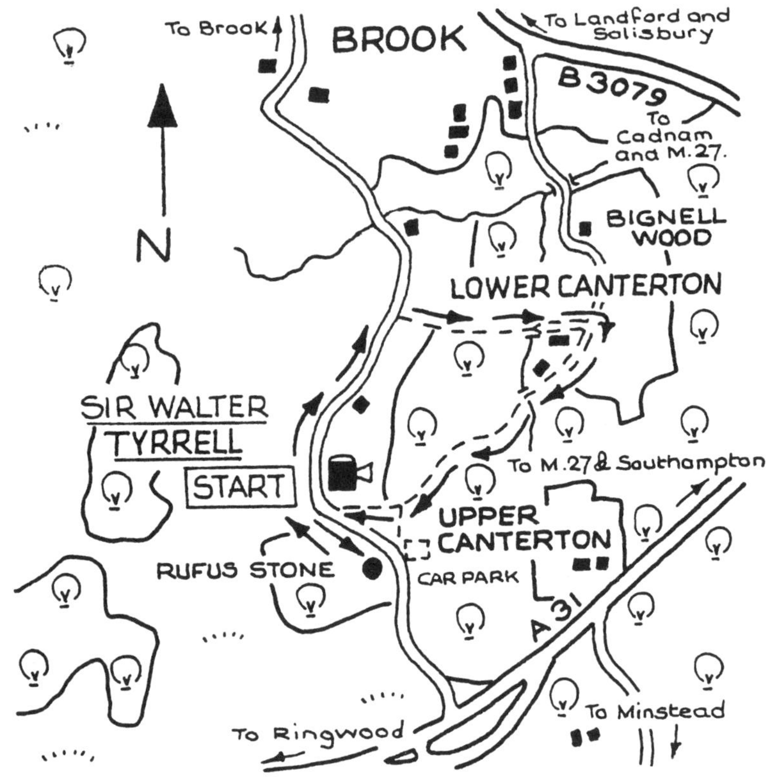

pened here on that fateful August day, give varied accounts of how the arrow actually struck the King. But one account is given on the side of the Stone: 'Here stood the oak tree on which an arrow shot by Sir Walter Tyrrell at a stag glanced and struck King William II on the breast of which he instantly died...' Was it an accident or was it murder? Tyrrell, who fled capture, always pleaded his innocence and was rewarded with lands by the new king, Henry II. Did this man really fire the arrow? Was it all arranged by Henry who had himself crowned only three days after his brother's death? Or was it some dispossessed Saxon or vengeful cleric whose property William had seized? We may never know the real answer, but there was one point everyone agreed upon. William II was the most detested of kings and his corpse would still be in Canterton Glen if a passing charcoal burner called Purkiss had not found his body and taken it in his cart for burial in Winchester along a route still named the King's road.

34

Return to the lane and cross over to the car park. Turn left along a little track signed 'Access to Cottage, please keep clear'. Follow this to see a real New Forest cottage, thatched, with 'dob' walls. Forest cottages had to be built with whatever came readily to hand. Clayey loam was mixed with heather, rushes or straw and then 'dobbed' or bonded by the builder with a three-pronged fork in successive layers on stone or brick foundations. The result was a snug home, warm in winter and cool in summer.

Turn left past the cottage to return past two Forestry Commission barriers to the lane. Turn right to walk down the grass-bordered lane past the pub which is on your right. The lane leads you deep into Canterton Glen between meadows golden with buttercups. When the lane bends left you will see a bridleway sign on the right. Leave the lane and turn right along the bridleway which is metalled at first and then becomes a woodland path, sunk deep between high banks entwined with tree roots. The path climbs through Pipers Copse, then drops to cross a tiny stream. (If this path is muddy, there is a narrow path on top of the bank on the left). A broad green way now leads ahead to the tiny hamlet of Lower Canterton.

This small group of houses, hidden away in the Forest glades and only approached by tracks, is a fascinating place. The houses are grouped in the ancient fashion, in a circle, surrounded by a high hedge. This was probably once surmounted by a stockade to defend the people against wild animals. The name gives a clue to its ancient origins. 'Canterton' means the village of the Kentish men. Jutish tribes were the first to settle in Kent and the New Forest after the departure of the Roman legions and before William the Conqueror's annexation of the Forest earned it its present name, this area was called Ytene or land of the Jutes.

Turn right to walk beside the hedge with the open forest on your left. The hedge, which becomes an embankment as it runs through woodland is now your guide. Pass the Forestry Commission barrier and keep on over the grass with the hedge close on your right. Cross a stream to enter woodland and now, although there is no clear path, it is not difficult to navigate. Continue, keeping the hedge, and later the embankment, as close as possible on your right. The woods give way to lawns and the embankment to a hedge again as you approach the old New Forest cottage you saw earlier in the walk. You will see its white walls over the hedge. Continue to the lane and turn right for the pub.

7 Pilley
The Fleur de Lys

Whitewashed half-timbered walls under a deep thatched roof make the Fleur de Lys everyone's idea of a typical English pub. It is the oldest pub in the Forest. Recent tests suggest that it probably dates back to the beginning of the 11th century! Originally it was a pair of Foresters' cottages, the tree roots and fireplace opening (Forest rights were attached to fireplaces) can still be seen in the stone-flagged entrance. Ham was smoked in the huge chimney and the chain and pulley at the chimney head are still there. The Jacob Armitage and Beverley of Arnwood bars were named after characters in Captain Marryat's famous book *Children of the New Forest.* What pleasanter way can there be to absorb the history of the Forest than to visit this delightful pub? You might even see the kinder of the pub's two ghosts — a little old lady in grey who potters about keeping an eye on things. Families are made specially welcome and there is a garden area for children. Dogs are welcome too.

The pub is open all day and meals are served from 12-2.30, 6-9.30 (7-9.30 on Sundays) and barbecues are held in the garden in summer from 4-9.30. Specialities include fresh fish, lobster, and roast pheasant in herb, port and red currant sauce. Cream teas are served from 3-5.30. Drinks are available all day from 11-11. Sundays 11-2.30 and 7-10.30. Real ales include Flowers and Boddingtons and the draught cider is Scrumpy Jack. There is an extensive wine list and a winter treat is mulled wine.

Cars can be left in the pub car park while you walk. Accommodation is available. Telephone 01590 672158

How to get there: Pilley is about 2 miles north of Lymington. Approaching from Lyndhurst, take the A337 Lymington road. Drive through Brockenhurst and after 3 miles turn left following the sign for Boldre. Drive through Boldre, cross the river and follow the minor road as it bears right then left for Pilley. The pub is on your right.

Parking: The pub car park.

Length of the walk: 2 miles. An easy ramble but be prepared for mud at times. Map: OS Outdoor Leisure 22 New Forest.

Although this walk is only two miles in length, it is delightfully varied. Meadow paths lead to one of the prettiest copses in the Forest, fragrant with bluebells in the spring. A ramble beside the Lymington river leads you back to the pub.

The Walk
With the front of the pub on your left, walk past the entrance to the car park. A footpath sign immediately after the car park indicates a narrow grassy path running left beside the fields. Turn left as the sign indicates, cross the stile and keep ahead with a hedge on your left. This fertile farming land around Pilley was originally owned by the de Redvers family who received large estates as a reward for their services from William the Conqueror. It was inherited by their kinsman, William de Vernum who supported the Dauphin of France in his vain attempt to wrest the English throne from King John. William's coat of arms included the Fleur de Lys which explains the name of the pub in this most English of villages!

Cross the stile to a grass-bordered country lane and turn left to follow it between high hedges which thin occasionally to give wide

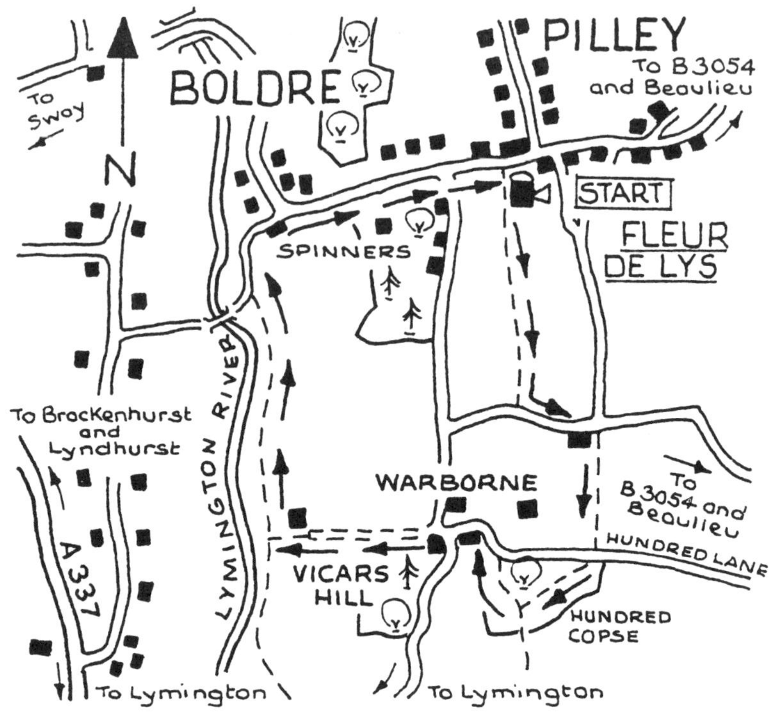

views over lush meadows to a wooded skyline. The lane passes Warborne Farm which is on the right, then bears left past some barns. Just past the barns look carefully for a footpath sign on the right. Turn right following the sign through two small iron gates and keep straight ahead as the path becomes a farm track and runs to meet Hundred Lane. Cross the lane and climb the steps ahead to go through a little wooden gate into Hundred Copse.

Follow the path through the copse, well-known for its bluebells. Most of the hazels and beeches have been coppiced to produce a mass of shoots allowing the flowers to flourish beneath them. A variety of woodland birds find ideal nesting sites here. The path runs through the trees, close to the edge of the wood to another small wooden gate. Go through to meet a crosspath. Turn right to take a wider green path which drops a little downhill through tangled woodland. A marshy area on the left is golden with irises in June.

A peaceful scene on the Lymington river near Pilley

When the path meets a lane, turn left to walk up to a junction. A circle of grassland shaded by an enormous oak tree stands to the left of the lane. We keep straight on here, ignoring the lane which leads left from the junction but before doing so, take a look at an elegant 18th century house, Gilpins, which stands on the corner. This was the home of William Gilpin who was presented with the living of Boldre (his parish included Pilley) in 1777. He spent much time exploring the New Forest and his books which included *Remarks on Forest Scenery* greatly influenced contemporary attitudes towards nature. The accepted 18th century view of wild countryside was that it was barbaric. Gilpin pointed out that it was beautiful, especially if it was 'picturesque'. He cared for his parishioners and with the proceeds from his books he built a school for them and endowed a poor house.

Cross straight over School Lane and continue ahead following the bridleway sign to the top of Vicars Hill. Now a lovely view of the valley of the Lymington river with its wooded hillsides opens before you. The track dips downhill under magnificent beech trees towards a white house. Keep straight ahead down some shallow concrete steps to the left of the house. The bridleway drops steeply downhill to the rush and flower-filled marshes that border the riverside. At the foot, turn right, with the river over the marsh on your left. This is a beautiful walk but be prepared for possible muddy patches. The wide valley was formed when the Lymington river was tidal and the marshes flooded at high water. In 1731, a merchant navy captain, William Cross, built a toll bridge dam with two sluices across the river, so that it was no longer navigable by large craft. He had acquired the rights to the mud flats from one Robert Pamplyn, Yeoman of the Robes to Charles I. Now, the river flows lazily through a jungle of bulrushes, irises and cow parsley.

Go through a wooden gate to meet another narrow leafy lane. Turn right to follow the lane which sinks deep beneath tree roots and runs to join a wider road. Turn right along the grass verge as the road climbs gently past some old cottages with attractive gardens. Just past the entrance to the vicarage look for a little footpath on the left which turns to run beneath the trees parallel with the road. Opposite School Lane, which is on your right, you pass the William Gilpin Primary school. If you have time you might like to follow School Lane for a short distance to visit Spinners Gardens. The path beside the road quickly brings you back to the pub which you will see ahead.

8 Emery Down
The New Forest Inn

Emery Down is less than a mile west of Lyndhurst but after the bustle of the Forest capital it seems to belong to a different world. Sheltered by dense oak and beech woods, the houses are dotted along a hillside, their gardens making a colourful patchwork in the dips and hollows. The New Forest Inn suits this old world atmosphere perfectly. In the early 1700s a caravan stood on the site, having claimed 'squatters' rights'. According to the law of the Forest, if you could build a house with a hearth before the authorities discovered it, then you could stay. As a licence to sell beer was not necessary at that time, a trader sold ale from the caravan. Today the caravan forms all of the front lounge porchway and can also be seen forming part of a bar wall.

Families are made very welcome inside and there is a woodland garden. Food is served from 11-9.30 Monday to Saturday, and during the usual drinking hours on Sunday. Delicious home-made dishes include a wide range of specials. I can recommend sauté of beef in Guinness with mushrooms, and rabbit in two-mustard sauce. For a sweet you could be tempted by a banana and butterscotch pavlova or simply strawberries and cream. Drinking hours are from 11-11 daily. (Sunday 12-10.30.) Real ales are Flowers Original, Strong Country, Wadworth 6X, Greene King, Abbot and Gales HSB. Strongbow draught cider and a wide range of wines are available.

Dogs are welcome. The licensee is happy to let customers leave cars in the car park while they walk but it is wise to enquire first as the pub does get very busy. If there is no room there is space beside the Bolderwood road on the left just past the pub.

Telephone: 01703 282329

How to get there: Approaching from Lyndhurst, follow the A35 (Bournemouth) road a short distance out of the village and turn right for Emery Down at Swan Green, opposite the Swan Inn. Drive through the village and the pub is on the left at the junction of two minor roads.

Parking: The pub car park, or beside the left-hand road (to Bolderwood and Fritham).

Length of the walk: 3 miles. Map: OS Outdoor Leisure 22 New Forest.

This short easy walk follows a ridge in the heart of the Forest and gives a rare insight into the Forest's beauty especially its contrasting shades of woodlands. It includes a spectacular viewpoint. If you wish to see the Forest as it was in the time of William the Conqueror without a house in sight or a suspicion of a road, then this walk is for you.

The Walk

With your back to the front of the pub and the road leading into the village on your right, take the road leading slightly uphill a little to your left. (Not the road sharp left signed for Bolderwood or the private drive on the left just beyond.) You may have to watch for traffic. The road runs past attractive houses and gardens. Continue for about a quarter of a mile past a joining lane on the right. Now look for a turning on the left, a few yards past a letter box. Leave the road and turn left up a gravel track and when it divides, take the right-hand track which leads past some houses

42

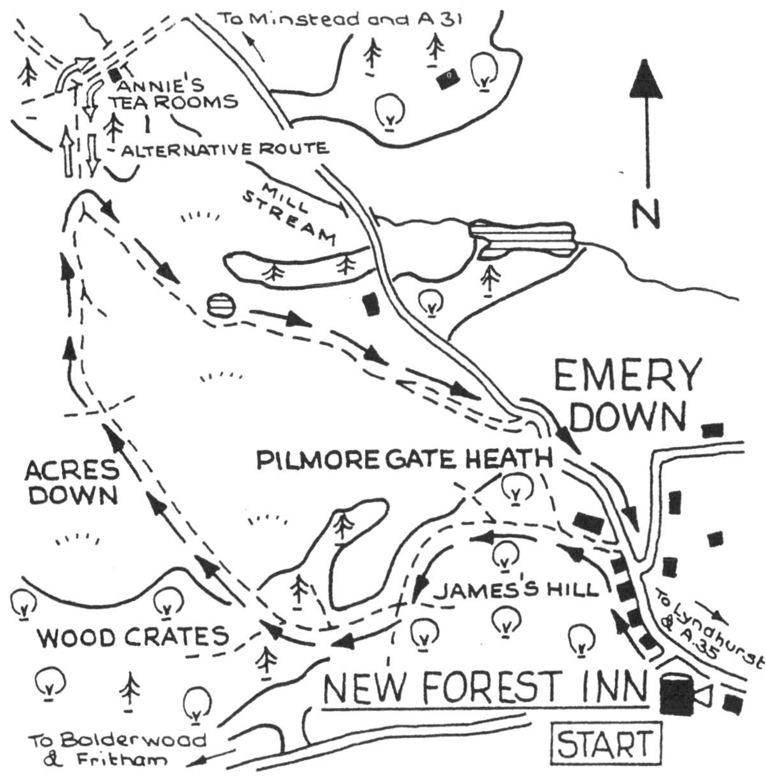

on the right. In front of the last house the gravel finishes, giving way to green Forest lawns. Turn right round the last house and follow the path over the grass. Continue along the same path into the oak and beech woods north of James's Hill. After about 60 yards the path divides. Keep ahead down the grassy left-hand path. Follow the path through the trees for about 80 yards to a more open area and be ready for some careful navigation! A path leads left down a small gully and marks our route. Turn left through the trees just before the gully and bear a little right to descend to a wide green clearing. Now the path is clearly visible continuing straight ahead over the grass towards the woods of Broom Hill Inclosure. When the path divides, continue straight ahead — the right-hand path. A beautiful path now leads through mixed woodlands of oak, beech, holly and silver birch.

*Boultbee's Cottages at Emery Down, almshouses endowed by
Admiral Boultbee in the mid-nineteenth century.*

This path curves round the foot of James's Hill. In the past the hill
was valued as it was one of the few isolated hills in the Forest which
still retained a thick gravel capping. On an old map of 1789 it is called
'gravel hill' and the former diggings can be seen on the top. Until
recent times, all important roads through the Forest were gravelled
and it is hard to believe that the present A35 was gravelled up to the
beginning of the second world war. Until late in the 19th century,
less important routes were mere mud tracks and coaches and
carriages had to be guided by postillions.

Ignore all side tracks until you come to a crossing path. Turn right
then keep to the main path as it bears left past a joining path on the
right. The path crosses a more open area then leads towards the trees
of Wood Crates. When the path divides, keep ahead along the right-
hand path. This remote heath is a favourite with fallow and roe deer.
Look for them closer to the trees at the edge as the lower ground is
too boggy for them. Waving tufts of cotton grass and the pungent
scent of bog myrtle give warning of this.

Now you can see our objective clearly. This is Acres Down, a high
heath and gorse-covered ridge rising ahead a little to your right.

Follow the path through the trees and cross a small stream. The path rises towards an open area and forks. Continue along the right-hand path which now leads directly towards Acres Down and climbs up the ridge. Wide views over billowing waves of woodland reward you as you climb to the top where you must pause and look back. The view over the heart of the Forest is really wonderful. Looking south, the blue curves of the Isle of Wight downs are etched on the skyline. The dark pines which contrast so vividly with the soft greens of the oak and beech woods mark the valley of Highland Water. Canadian troops camped here as they awaited the D-Day landings and this pine-clad valley reminded them of home.

Follow the main path across Acres Down, ignoring all side tracks, until you come to a well-defined crosstrack. Keep to the main path as it turns right along the top of the ridge. After about a quarter of a mile you pass a joining track on the right. Ignore this and keep ahead as the path dips and continues through a wooded area. After a few yards you will see a green path on your right which leads along the side of a valley, over Pilmore Gate Heath. This is our way, but if you would like tea in very pleasant surroundings keep on and when you meet a crosstrack turn left downhill. Annie's tea room is at the foot of the hill.

To continue the walk turn right as directed above or, if you have had tea, retrace your steps and turn left. The path rambles along the valley and after about 100 yards bear a little left downhill to see a small pond which is covered in cream and scarlet waterlilies in June. The path becomes a wide gravelled track and leads back to the minor road. Turn right to walk back to the New Forest Inn.

9 High Corner
The High Corner Inn

This pub beside an old drovers' track in the quieter more remote countryside in the north of the Forest is not easy to find, but, as I am sure you will discover, it is well worth the effort. The northern Forest is crossed by valleys carved by small streams flowing into the Avon. High Corner Inn nestles against a wooded hillside overlooking one of the most attractive of these streams — Dockens Water. The pub is low, rambling and picturesque. Built originally as a farmhouse in the early 1700s, many additions over the centuries have provided room for everyone, especially families. You can eat in one of three family rooms if you wish, there is plenty of indoor seating for children, a Lego room and a woodland garden with an adventure playground.

Meals are served in the bar or restaurant daily at lunchtime and in the evenings till 10. On Sunday there is a carvery in the bar 12-2.30 and in the restaurant from 12-3.30. Mouth-watering dishes include such delights as homemade venison, bacon and stout pie and half a roast lemon chicken with coleslaw and garlic dip. Children have

46

their own special menu. In summer, drinking hours are from 11-3 and 6-11 Monday to Friday. Saturday 11-11. In winter the hours are from 11-2.30 and 7-10.30 (11 on Friday). Saturday 11-3 and 6-11. Normal drinking hours are observed on Sunday. Real ales available are Boddingtons, Wadworth 6X and Flowers. Cider (Taunton Dry and Woodpecker Medium Sweet) and a full range of wines are on offer. Dogs will find their brew in the garden.

Cars can be left in one of the large car parks. For a longer stay, accommodation is available.

Telephone: 01425 473973.

How to get there: The best approach is from Lyndhurst. Take the A35 through Lyndhurst in the direction of Bournemouth. Turn left from the bypass, and take the next road on the right opposite the Swan Inn signed for Emery Down. Just past the New Forest Inn bear left along the road signed for Bolderwood. The road heads west then north under the A31. Ignore all side tracks and continue to the High Corner Inn sign indicating a track on the right. Turn right as directed and drive down to the Inn which is on the left.

Parking: In the pub car park.

Length of the walk: 3 miles. Map: OS Outdoor Leisure 22 New Forest.

This is an easy stroll in one of the most out-of-the-way places in the Forest. Dockens Water flows through a beautifully-wooded valley and a gentle climb is rewarded by superb views.

The Walk

With your back to the front of the Inn, bear left past a turning on the left and keep ahead down a gravel track shaded by fine oak trees. Protected from grazing animals by their understorey of holly, some of these giants show the effects of pollarding — sprouting several thick branches from a shortened trunk. Keep to the main track past a thatched house on the left. The track bears right over grassy lawns to descend into the valley with wooded hillsides rising ahead. Ignore a track on the left which leads to a bridge and follow the main track as it turns more sharply right to lead past Woodford Bottom car park. Keep ahead past the Forestry Commission barrier to walk through

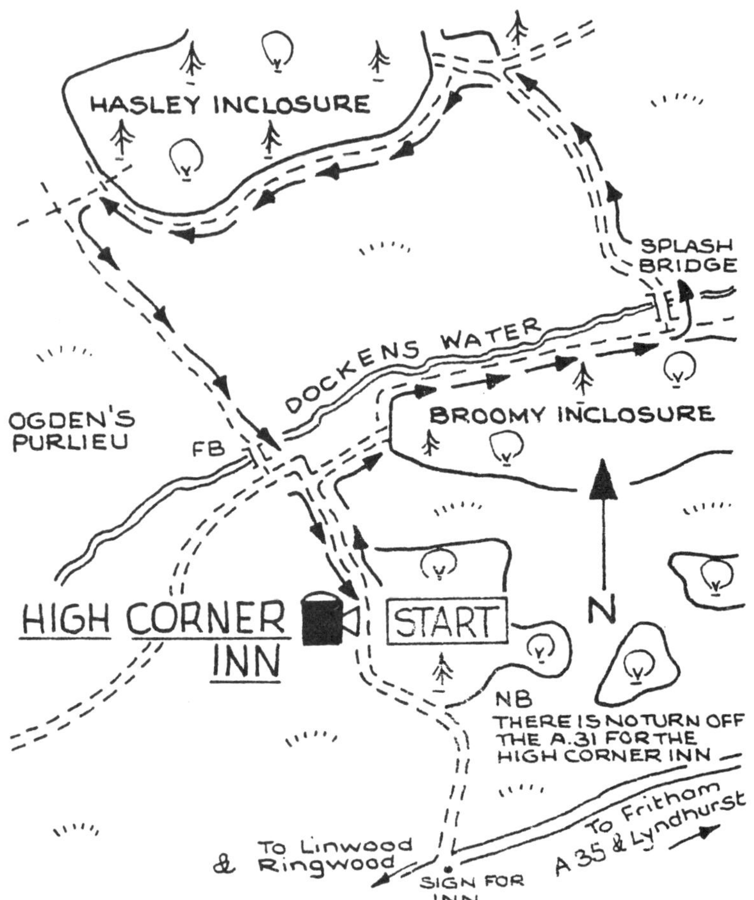

more fine oak woodland to a gate. Do not go through the gate, but, just before it, turn left over the grass with a wire fence on your right. After a few yards turn right (the fence turns right at this point) to follow a beautiful green path beside the fence along the valley. Dockens Water curves through banks hung with ferns a few yards over the grass on your left. The thick woods of the inclosure on the right are home to badgers. Wooden 'badger gates' have been made under the fence to allow them to follow their accustomed paths to the stream. You can trace their footprints to a small pebble beach by the waterside.

The path follows the valley for almost a mile to a crosstrack. Turn left over the grass to cross a small bridge over Dockens Water. Ahead rise bracken and heather-covered hillsides and outlined against the sky on the right are the tree-covered slopes of Sloden Inclosure, a mysterious wood hiding the remains of a lost village and Romano-British potteries. Follow the white track ahead as it climbs the hillside towards the trees of Hasley Inclosure. As you near the top you will see the gate into the inclosure ahead. Do not go through the gate, but, about 50 yards before it, turn left along a narrow path that runs along the hillside with the inclosure fence close on the right. The path traces the hillside for almost a mile and all the way you can enjoy glorious views over the valley of Dockens Water and the unspoilt northern Forest. Do not take any of the smaller paths running downhill but keep the inclosure fence on your right.

When the inclosure fence turns right, keep it as your guide and turn right in line with it. Ahead you will see a conspicuous grove of dark pine trees. Follow the path to a point just past the pines where a barred track leads into the wood on the right. Turn left, the pines are on your left, to a crossing track. Turn left again along the track, the pines are still on your left, and follow the path as it winds its way downhill towards a long, low thatched house in the valley. As you near the house, Ogdens Purlieu, you will see that it is reminiscent of a Saxon farmstead with its single-storey wings and low thatch over a rounded arched doorway. You will find purlieus in various parts of the Forest. Purlieu is of course a French word, dating back to William the Conqueror and derived from 'pour allez' — to walk round an area. This land was once subject to Forest laws and reserved for the deer but by special dispensation it was later allowed to be enclosed and cultivated. At the crosstrack in the valley, bear left for a few yards then walk over the grass to cross a wooden footbridge over Dockens Water. This leads to the gravel track taken at the beginning of the walk. Bear a little right to follow it uphill to High Corner Inn which is on the right.

10 Wootton
The Rising Sun Inn

Wootton village is now on the southern boundary of the New Forest but in the past when the Forest extended to the coast it was a lonely, isolated settlement in wild moorland, a haunt of smugglers and highwaymen. The Rising Sun Inn, only a few miles from an ancient smuggling 'run' up Beckton Bunny, was a favourite port of call for the free traders as it was for other travellers. It is said that for many years the French brandy sold there came free of duty!

The inn was rebuilt in Victorian times and has recently been restored retaining many original features including the stained glass windows and doors. Inside there is a plush Victorian Bar with a splendid open fireplace. The alcoves provide plenty of room for families and the pub prides itself on its efforts to please children who have their own menu including scaled-down versions of their parents' meals. Delicious fare includes steak and stout casserole, stuffed plaice, leek and smoky bacon bake and braised venison.

The inn is open for meals all day from 10-11 (12-10.30 on Sunday). Drinking hours are from 11 am-11 pm with normal hours on Sunday. Real ales include Flowers, Boddingtons, Ringwood Best Bitter and Whitbread, there is Scrumpy Jack cider on tap and an extensive wine list.

Beautiful Forest views can be enjoyed from the garden and children have their own fenced play area with an animal paddock close by, with horses, donkeys, pigs and goats. Walkers are welcome to bring their dogs and leave their cars. Accommodation is available for a longer stay.

Telephone: 01425 610360

How to get there: The Inn is easily reached from the main A35 Bournemouth-Southampton road. Travelling from Lyndhurst, drive for about 6 miles and turn left along the B3058 signed for Milford-on-Sea, New Milton, Wootton, Bashley and Tiptoe. In just over a mile as the road turns right for Bashley, you will see the Inn across the road on the corner.

Parking: In the large pub car park.

Length of the walk: 2 ¹/₂ miles. Map: OS Outdoor Leisure 22 New Forest.

This is a beautiful walk in a quiet part of the Forest, mostly over open heaths but part of the return route follows grassy paths through a woodland inclosure. The highlight of the walk is the lovely valley of Avon Water.

The Walk

Return to the road from the Rising Sun car park and turn right, leaving the front of the Inn on your right, following the sign for Sway and Lymington. Keep straight on towards the Sway road, the B3055, past the junction with a minor road to Brockenhurst. Continue along the narrow path which runs over the grass to the left of the B3055. The path runs parallel with the road for about a quarter of a mile, over a typical Forest 'lawn' — a large grassy plain cropped short by the many Forest ponies who live in this peaceful area. As the road marks the southern boundary of the Forest it is interesting to compare its open heaths and woodland, still presenting in many respects a medieval landscape, with the neatly-hedged farming land just a few yards away.

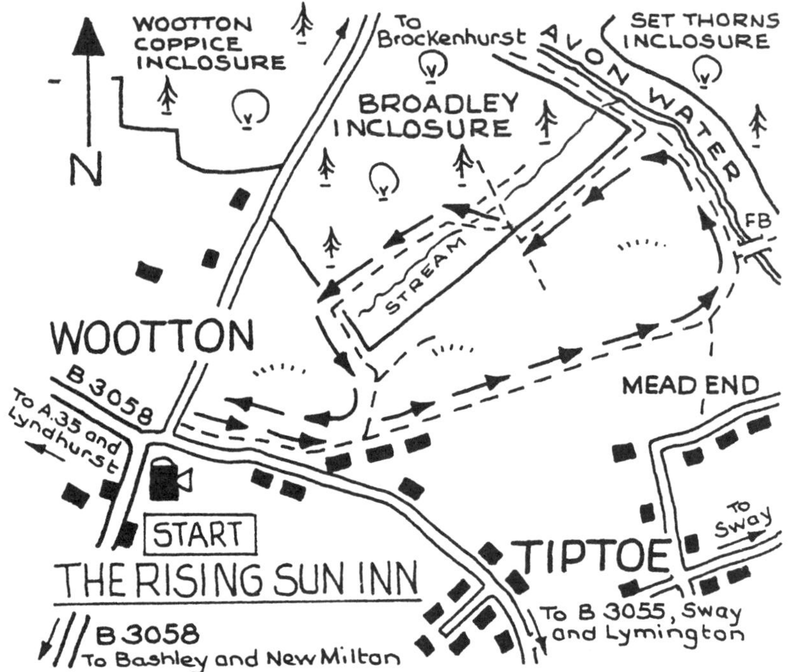

As the path bears a little left over the heath the road disappears behind a belt of trees. You pass a small wood on the left (the path to the right of the wood is our return route) and as the path dips slightly, the view ahead changes dramatically. The flat heath gives way to your first sight of the wooded hillsides of the valley of Avon Water. Follow the path as it slopes gently downhill into the valley to meet another path and bears slightly left towards a scattering of trees. Walk through the trees to one of the most attractive places in the New Forest, the green lawns fringing Avon Water, west of Set Thorns Inclosure. The tree-shaded stream flows briskly round small pebble beaches between banks hung with ferns. Wetland plants, including the aromatic bog myrtle, golden waterlilies and sundew flourish here. Captain Marryat set his *Children of the New Forest* in this area and it is easy to imagine Jacob Armitage's cottage in this romantic valley.

A small wooden footbridge crosses the stream ahead. Do not cross, but just before the bridge turn left along the path through the trees fringing the left bank of the stream. Continue for only a few yards then bear a little left away from the stream towards more open grassland. Keep ahead with the streamside trees on your right.

The path becomes indistinct as you walk through the glades but there are no problems with navigation as the stream runs close on your right the whole way. Shortly the path becomes clear again and the trees on the right part to reveal a ford. Walk straight ahead towards the fence marking the edge of Broadley Inclosure. Turn left at the fence and follow the good path running to the left of the inclosure boundary. On your right the wood is fringed by a magnificent sequence of Scots pines, their flaking russet bark overlaid in patterns like wave marks on a beach.

When you come to a crosstrack, you will see a gate leading into the inclosure on the right. Turn right, through the gate, then turn immediately left off the main track, to follow a green path which runs diagonally through the wood. Cross a footbridge over a small stream and keep ahead over a more open area to a crosspath. Turn left to follow a wide grassy ride, shaded by tall pines, oaks and beeches. Broadley Inclosure is secluded and peaceful and there is a good chance of seeing deer. Ignore all side tracks and keep ahead. The path rises a little under an archway of spreading oak tree boughs and continues over crosstracks to a gate leading out of the inclosure. Go through the gate and turn left with the inclosure boundary now on your left. The path leads downhill over two tiny streams before rising slightly. When the boundary fence turns left, keep straight on with a small wood on your right to a crosspath. Bear right and over the heath on your left you will see the path you followed from the inn at the beginning of the walk. Cross the heath to the path and retrace your steps to The Rising Sun.

 # Lyndhurst, Clay Hill
The Crown Stirrup

Over 300 years old, The Crown Stirrup has the cosy atmosphere of a real Forest home. There is no stone in the Forest and old houses had to be built with whatever came to hand. The oak beam in the lounge bar was originally a ship's timber from Bucklers Hard where many great warships were built in the past. The name is also linked with the history of the Forest as it refers to the Rufus Stirrup, which hangs in the Verderers' Hall in Lyndhurst, dating not from Norman times as you might expect but from the 17th century. Only the King could hunt the deer in the Forest and any Forest Commoner's dog too large to pass through the stirrup iron had to have its claws clipped or 'expeditated'.

Families are welcome and there is plenty of room for children inside. The pretty garden where drinks can be taken on the terrace, is enclosed and children have their own play area with a tree house. Tempting meals are served lunchtimes from 11-2.30 and evenings from 6-11. (Sunday from 12-3 and 7-10.30.) Specialities include venison in cranberry and port sauce, sauté of rabbit in mustard sauce and Mediterranean vegetable and cheese Wellington. Children have their own menu. Wines are a speciality and house wines are available by the glass out of the bottle. The pub is open for drinking throughout the year from 11-3 and 5.30-11. On Sunday normal drinking hours are observed. Real ales include 6X, Flowers and Boddingtons. The draught cider is Bulmer's Original.

Dogs on leads are welcome, and cars can be left in the car park while you walk.

Telephone: 01703 282272

How to get there: Leave Lyndhurst on the A337 (Brockenhurst) road. After about a quarter of a mile, just past a sign for Foxlease House on the right, you will see The Crown Stirrup to the left of the road.

Parking: In the pub car park.

Length of the walk: 2 $^{1}/_{4}$ miles. Map: OS Outdoor Leisure 22 New Forest.

The New Forest historian, John Wise, wrote in 1883 'The people of Lyndhurst ought, I always think, to be the happiest and most contented in England, for they possess a wider park and nobler trees than even royalty.' He could say the same today. This walk explores two of the great woods he would recognise near the village, Pondhead Inclosure and Park Ground Inclosure. It also includes a stroll along The Ridge east of the village giving wide Forest views. This walk starts directly from the pub garden and the landlord will give you details of a shorter walk if you wish.

The Walk

Leave the pub garden by the small wooden gate just past the children's play area. Turn left and you are immediately surrounded by Forest, following a good path beneath the fine oak and beech trees of Park Ground Inclosure. Go through a gate opening to a gravel crosstrack which runs left to Beechen Lane. Cross straight over the track and through the gate on the other side. A woodland path leads ahead along the edge of Pondhead Inclosure. These old woods allow plenty of light to filter through their branches and the glades are carpeted with bluebells in late spring and bright with

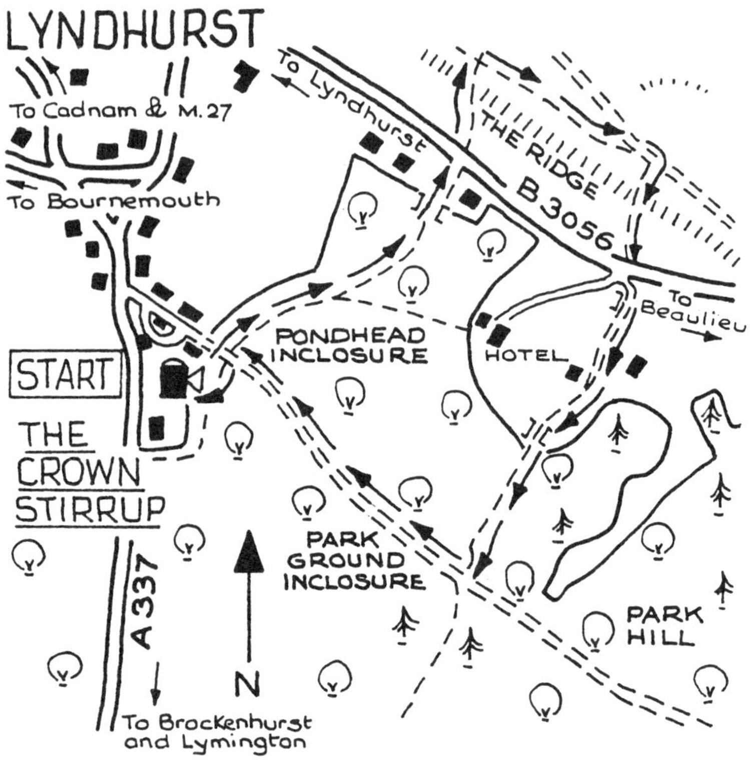

foxgloves in summer. When the path divides, continue along the left-hand path. Look carefully to the left after about 100 yards for a plaque on a small wooden support. The area behind the plaque is known as 'William's Copse'. Nine hundred sessile oaks were planted here in 1979 'to commemorate the creation of the New Forest by William I in 1079'.

The path leads over a wooden bridge to a gate. Go through and keep ahead to the next gate with a stile which leads out of the inclosure. Follow the track directly ahead to the B3056 Lyndhurst-Beaulieu road. Cross straight over, go past the Forestry Commission barrier and climb the path ahead up the heath-covered slope to the top of The Ridge. From here there are wide views west to Lyndhurst church spire which rises from among the surrounding trees as a beacon to the traveller. To the north and east lie the great woods of

Matley and Denny. You cross a low earth embankment which forms the northern boundary of Lyndhurst Old Park Pale, a deer inclosure dating from the end of the 13th century. After crossing the embankment turn right along a green way leading close beside it. Continue for about a quarter of a mile as the wide way becomes a narrow path between the gorse bushes, still keeping the embankment close on the right. The path bears a little left to join a wider stony track. Bear right for only a few yards to a narrow path leading right, over the embankment. Turn right and follow the clear white path as it descends the heath, bearing a little left to the Lyndhurst-Beaulieu road. You will see a large red hotel sign on the opposite side of the road.

Cross the road and take the left-hand of the two metalled lanes ahead. This leads a little downhill, then curves right over a bridge to run between high hedges as a gravelled lane. Follow the lane to an open Forest lawn and keep straight on past a house. The path enters woods and becomes indistinct, but there is no difficulty with navigation. On the right you will see a wire inclosure fence. Keep ahead through the trees with the fence a few yards away on your right. Follow the line of the fence and after a short distance the path becomes clearer. The path bears a little left to cross a small wooden bridge. Do not bear left at this point but keep ahead with the fence still as your guide, a few yards away on your right. This is a beautiful walk through the oak and beech woods of Pondhead Inclosure. You are really in the heart of the Forest and there is every chance of seeing deer.

Through the trees ahead you will see a gravel crosstrack. Turn right along the gravel and follow this wide straight way leading between Park Ground Inclosure and Pondhead Inclosure. High deer fences run along their boundaries. Some fine pollarded beech trees shade the path as it dips to cross a stream and then rises a little to a gate which opens into Beechen Lane. Go through the gate and turn left through the small wooden gate leading to the path you followed near the start of the walk. Retrace your steps along the edge of Park Ground Inclosure to the gate on the right leading into the pub garden. The pub's name, The Crown Stirrup is on the gate.

⓬ Nomansland
The Lamb Inn

The Lamb Inn overlooks the northern border of the Forest at the point where it follows the county boundary. The Inn is in Wiltshire but the front steps are in Hampshire. Formerly the border ran through the pub itself and as closing time was earlier in Hampshire, everyone moved across into the Wiltshire bar at the appropriate time! It is a friendly, welcoming pub where you will quickly feel part of Forest life. From the bay windows you look across wide lawns grazed by Forest ponies to the beech woods of Bramshaw Inclosure. Families have plenty of room to spread themselves inside and there is a garden.

Delicious meals are served every day from 12-2.30 and 6.30-10 except Sunday when the hours are 7-9. There is something to satisfy everyone whether content with a snack — perhaps prawn salad with Marie Rose sauce — or feeling like something more substantial such as home-made steak 'n ale pie. If you attempt the mixed grill (steak, liver, chop, gammon and kidney) I suggest you do the walk first! Sweets on offer include home-made apple, cherry and apricot pie. There is a special menu for children. Drinking hours are from 11-3 and 6-11 Monday to Friday, 11-11 Saturday, and 12-3 and 7-10.30 on Sunday. Real ales include Ringwood, 6X and Boddingtons Mild. The draught cider is Inchs' Stonehouse. Wines are sold by glass or bottle.

Well-behaved dogs on leads are welcome and walkers are free to leave cars in the large parking area opposite the pub.

Telephone: 01794 390246.

How to get there: From the Cadnam roundabout (M27 junction 1) take the B3079 in the direction of Bramshaw and Landford. Bear right in Brook past the junction with the B3078 and in just over 2 miles turn left for Nomansland. When the roads divides keep straight on over the green to the Lamb Inn which you will see over the road directly ahead.

Parking: Beside the pub or in the parking area beside the green. At busy times park in one of the car parks either side of the road.

Length of the walk: 2 miles but allow extra time as the route is rather hilly. Map: OS Outdoor Leisure 22 New Forest.

The beech trees in Bramshaw Inclosure were famous as early as the 13th century when they provided much of the timber used in Salisbury Cathedral. Most of this walk follows quiet ways through these lovely woods to climb to a viewpoint overlooking the Wiltshire downs.

The Walk

With your back to the front of the pub, walk down the road directly ahead over the green. On the left is the Well of Sacrifice, a memorial to the fallen in both World Wars, built on the site of the original village well. The great beeches of Bramshaw Inclosure arch overhead as you pass Nomansland Green car park on the left. Continue along the road and turn right to walk across the next car park, Bramshaw Wood. Beyond the right-hand corner of the car park you will see a good path leading ahead with an embankment close on the right. Take this path as it runs downhill beside the embankment which is our guide for the first part of the walk. When the path divides take the right-hand path to a crosstrack. Bear left for a few

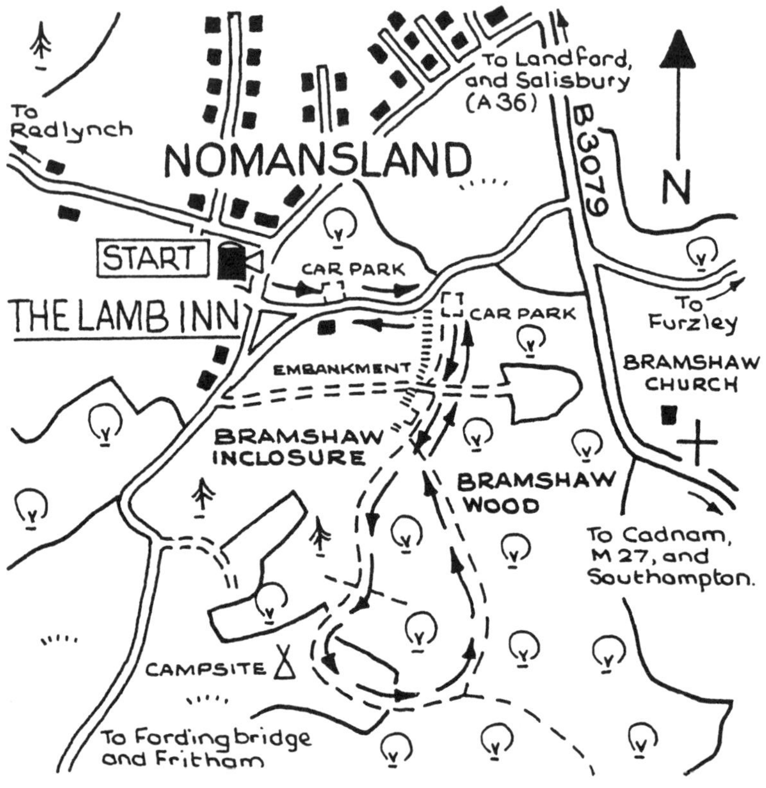

yards and then right to continue along the valley still following the line of the embankment. Cross a stream and continue past a joining path on the left which is the return route.

Keep ahead, ignoring all side paths as the route begins to rise a little. Slopes planted with oaks and beeches rise either side with here and there the massive many-boughed form of an ancient pollard. These woods were one of the last refuges of the gypsies. When they were married in Bramshaw church they were described as being 'of the Forest'. The woods also provided shelter for the Nomansland smugglers. It is said that they once concealed £100 worth of brandy in 40 kegs in a barn at Cadnam. Home they went, happily unaware they had been spotted. When they returned to collect their haul they found nothing. Heartbroken, they disbanded on the spot!

Cross a stream in a deep gully and keep ahead, still keeping the embankment on the right. The path begins to rise again and now bears a little left away from the embankment to more open glades. When you meet a crosstrack, bear slightly right to continue uphill through groups of very old silver-barked beeches. The path steepens as it nears the top to emerge from the trees by a Forestry Commission barrier. The open area ahead is used as a campsite. Walk over the site for a few yards, then bear left past the chemical disposal point to follow a narrow path over an embankment. Follow the path as it leads round the head of a valley. On the left the dense line of the Bramshaw woods falls away to give a magnificent view over folds of massed woodlands to the Wiltshire downs. This is an ideal spot for a picnic.

Continue along the path past a faint grassy track on the left. About 30 yards further on turn left down a well-defined white path. Follow this over the heath to enter the trees again and drop steeply downhill. Keep to the main path as it bears slightly left through beautiful mixed woods of oak, beech, birch and holly. These sunny woods are home to a wealth of wildlife including all species of our native woodpeckers. This is the New Forest at its best!

A track joins on the left which is the route you followed earlier from Bramshaw Wood car park. Retrace your steps, keeping the embankment on the left, to the car park. Turn left to follow the road back across the green to the Lamb Inn.

You might be intrigued by the name of Nomansland. It seems that for a long time no one was quite certain whether the land was within the perambulation of the Forest or not. When would-be residents claimed squatter's rights in accordance with Forest law, the authorities pulled the buildings down. But in 1800 the New Forest Commissioners relented and allowed houses to be built. A more romantic reason is provided by H M Lievens, writing in *The Salisbury Journal* in 1910, who says the village was founded by a gypsy in the 18th century. Other unmarried men joined him and they wooed brides from neighbouring villages to join them in their landlord-less paradise. In which case the name should surely be Nowomansland!

⓭ East End
The East End Arms

This homely, traditional-style pub is a real find. Tucked away down quiet country lanes with a pleasant shaded garden, The East End Arms offers a genuine Forest atmosphere, good food and a warm welcome to families. The bar area is completely separate from the rest of the pub. Home-cooked meals are served throughout the week — lunchtimes from 12-3 and in the evenings from 6.30-9.30. This is a 'game' pub and as well as venison you can try pheasant or perhaps pigeon pie. Other examples of the hearty country fare on offer include steak-and-Guinness pie and faggots. Delicious sweets include Spotted Dick, treacle pudding and apricot crumble.

Drinking hours are from 11.30-3 and from 6-11 with normal Sunday opening times. Ringwood and Adnams are two of the dozen or more real ales available. Draught cider is on tap and there is an extensive wine list. Dogs are allowed in the bar and in the garden but should be on a lead. Visitors are welcome to leave their cars while they walk. Incidentally, I am told that the stocks you will see in the garden are hardly ever used!

Telephone: 01590 626223

How to get there: From Lyndhurst take the A337 Lymington road. Approaching Brockenhurst, turn left along the B3055 Beaulieu road for four and a half miles. Turn right along the B3054 beside Hatchet Pond for a few yards then turn left for East Boldre. Continue south to a crossroads and turn right to drive through East End village, past the turning to Norleywood to the pub which is on the left of the road.

Parking: In the pub car park.

Length of the walk: 2 miles. Map: OS Outdoor Leisure 22 New Forest

This is an interesting walk between two worlds. East End is a small Forest hamlet built along the boundary of the Beaulieu Manor Estate. The Estate is now private land. The area around Beaulieu was granted originally to the monks of Beaulieu Abbey by King John and was bought by Lord Montagu's ancestors at the dissolution of the monasteries. Most of the houses face away from the Estate and look west across the open Forest where their animals could find pasture. The pub is south of the village and now overlooks land outside the New Forest boundary, so on this walk you will find footpath signs indicating rights-of-way which, of course, are generally not needed in the Forest where you can walk almost at will. The walk includes a particularly beautiful woodland path through Sowley Brooms.

The Walk
With your back to the pub turn left along the lane. The road divides in front of a grassy triangle. Take the left-hand lane and continue for just a few yards past a house and a letter box. Before you come to the road ahead you will see a small wooden gate on the left with a footpath sign and a Solent Way sign. Turn left through the gate along a wide field path. This part of the walk follows the Solent Way, a long-distance coastal footpath running east from near Christchurch to Emsworth. The coast is less than a mile away over the fields on the right and from here you can see the line of the Isle of Wight downs etched across the horizon.

Follow the path over stiles towards the trees of Sowley Brooms. Double stiles lead to a grassy path running through the sunny glades of this ancient oak wood. Keep on to a crosstrack. Leave the Solent

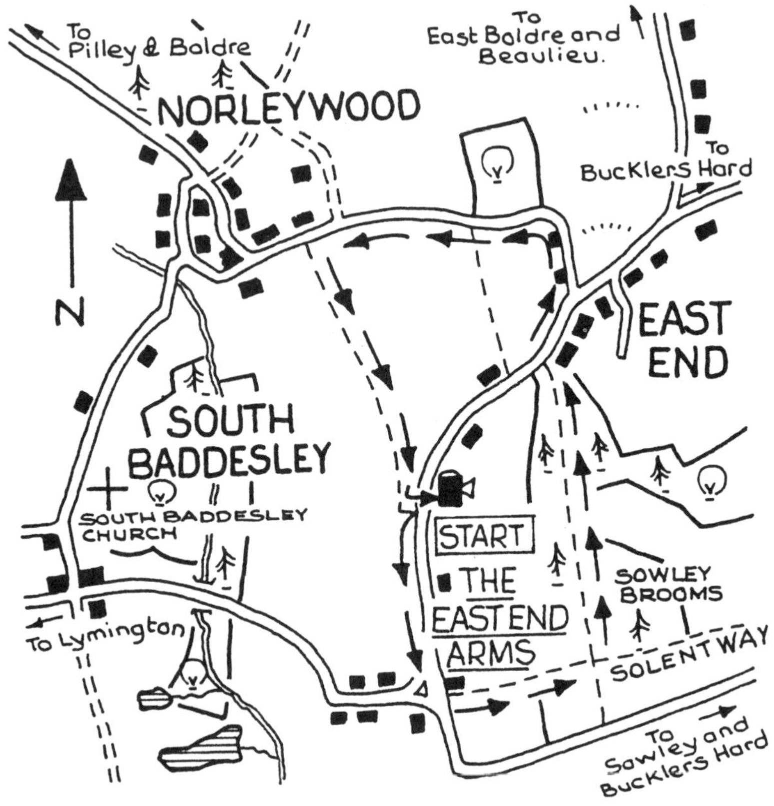

Way and turn left to take a wide path deeper into this glorious wood. It is a very quiet and remote place and you may see the shyer Forest animals, deer, foxes or badgers. Butterflies thrive in these oak woods and beside the path woodland flowers include orchids and the blue- and pink-flowered lungwort.

When the path leaves the wood in front of a more open area, bear a little left to cross a stile. The path now bears left over the grass to double stiles. Cross these and keep on over a field to go over another stile to a minor road. Turn right to cross East End bridge and walk up to a road junction. Turn left for Norleywood village. Open Forest land lies to the right of the road and makes pleasant walking. The road curves left past old cob cottages, made in the traditional fashion by bonding mud, straw and heather. Use of local materials made it

In Norleywood village

simpler for would-be Forest residents in the past to construct a home unnoticed by the authorities. If this could be achieved and a hearth constructed, they could claim squatters' rights and not be evicted. This explains the rambling nature of Forest villages! Just past the corner look for an attractive pond on the right. It is fringed with bulrushes and is almost covered with white-flowered waterlilies in summer.

Follow the lane as it becomes wooded either side. Ignore the first footpath sign you will see on the left and keep on to the first houses in Norleywood village. Pass a gravel track on the right and a few yards further on you will see a footpath sign on the left beside a stile and a gate. Turn left over the stile and follow the wide, fenced path straight ahead. Attractive farming country surrounds you with comfortable -looking farmhouses half-hidden in folds of woodland. Cross a stile and keep ahead with a hedge on your left. Just past a house close to the path look for a stile on the left. Cross the stile and walk the few yards to the lane followed at the start of the walk. (The last few yards may be overgrown but they are passable). Turn left to walk back to the East End Arms.

Godshill
The Fighting Cocks

The Fighting Cocks is a traditional country pub in beautiful heathland surroundings close to the high western rim of the New Forest above the Avon valley. The pub takes its name from the cockpit, a shallow depression visible on the other side of the road near the pond. The present pub was built in 1927 on the site of an old thatched inn. I was told that during the first World War the inn became a popular refuge for the troops stationed nearby. At closing time the RSM rode into the bar on his horse, sword in hand, and drove everyone back to camp! Times may have changed but the warm welcome has not and there is special consideration for families who have their own room.

Meals are served all week, lunchtimes from 12-2 and evenings 7-9.30. A wide selection is on offer from a Light Bite — perhaps crispy coated mushrooms with salad or a ploughmans — to a more substantial meal from the evening menu which includes some succulent chicken dishes such as chicken breasts filled with ham and cheese. From the tempting desserts we selected hot chocolate fudge cake and apple and blackberry crumble. Normal drinking hours are observed on Sundays and the rest of the week the pub is open from 11-2.30 and from 6-11. Real ales include Flowers, 6X and Speckled Hen. Strongbow cider is on tap.

Dogs on leads are welcome in the bar and garden and there is plenty of room to leave your car while you walk.

Telephone: 01425 652462

How to get there: From the Cadnam roundabout (M27 junction 1) take the B3079 in the direction of Bramshaw. Just past the Bell Inn in Brook take the Fordingbridge Road, B3078. In 3 miles the road divides. Continue along the B3078, left-hand road, for another 3 miles to Godshill and the pub is on the right.

Parking: Pub car park.

Length of the walk: 3 miles or 2 ½ by the shorter route. Map: OS Outdoor Leisure 22 New Forest.

An Iron Age hill fort crowning a wooded spur above the Avon valley is the highlight of this superb walk. But you will also enjoy wide moorland views and quiet ways through oak and beech woods. The return route for the longer walk (more attractive scenically) involves fording a shallow stream — no problem in wellies — but there is an alternative shorter route.

The Walk
With the front of the pub on your right, turn right down the Woodgreen Road. Pass a bridleway sign on the right and continue down the road for about 100 yards to a footpath sign on the left. Turn left and cross the stile ahead to follow a clear path with a hedge on the left. This attractive way leads over a field and as you approach the other end look for a small stile on the left. Bear left over this stile, and the one immediately after, and bear right to continue down a field with the hedge now on your right. Cross the next stile and keep ahead past a footpath on the left. The path here is lovely now running between high hedges bordered by wild flowers. Opposite a house the path divides. Take the left-hand path and follow it for only a few yards as it curves slightly downhill. You will see a footpath sign on the right. Turn right and follow a narrow path that drops steeply downhill through an oak and beech wood. The path winds

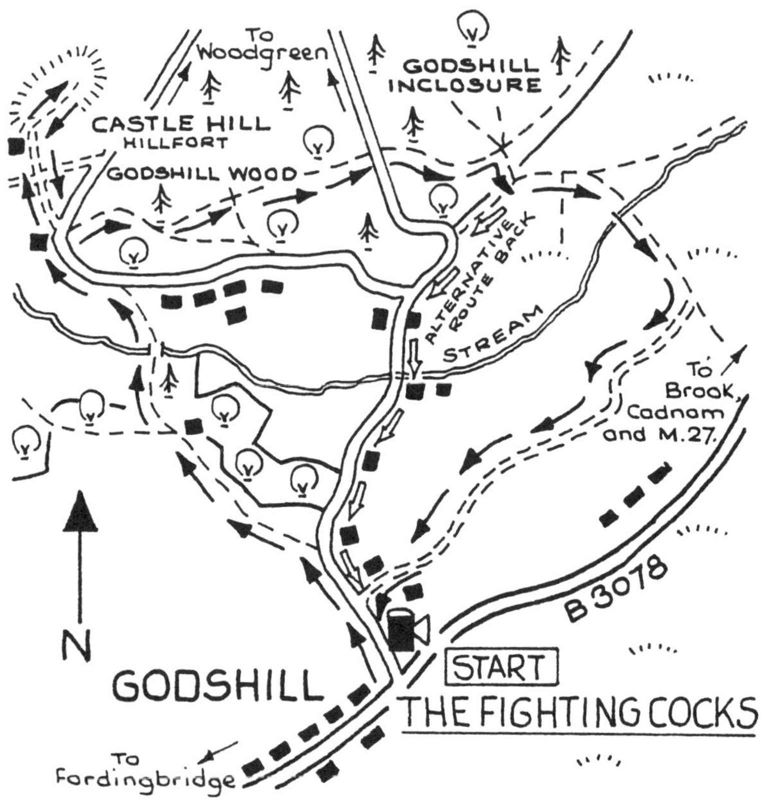

a little to make the descent less steep but there are helpful yellow waymarks on the trees. As you near the foot of the hill a footpath sign indicates a right turn through open glades to the bank of the stream threading the valley.

In front of the stream, turn left for a yard or two and bear right over the wooden footbridge. A good path leads ahead, at first between hedges and later over Forest lawns, past some cottages to meet a minor road. Continue beside the road as it curves right. Pass the entrance to a house close to the road on the left and immediately afterwards leave the road and turn left up the green path leading steeply uphill. You are scaling the side of Castle Hill Iron Age fort. Go straight over a crosstrack and continue uphill to a house on the left. In front of the house bear right for a few yards, then turn left to climb the embankment and reach the smooth green lawn that forms the central area of the fort. This is a magical place, remote and wooded and it is easy to imagine Celtic tribesmen standing here over 2000 years ago deciding that this cliff above the Avon valley would be an ideal defensive position. They would have crowned the embankments with timber ramparts. Trees obscure the view of the valley from the fort so walk over the central area and continue over more ditches and embankments towards the minor road where the trees thin to give you a superb view far over the Avon valley to the Wiltshire downs. At your feet the river winds through meadows past old mills and mellowed brick cottages.

Retrace your steps across the fort, turning right at the foot of the first descent, left past the house, over the crosspath and down the grassy path to the minor road. Cross the road and go through the gate into Godshill Wood. Follow the path ahead as it winds up through this pleasant mixed woodland of oak, beech, holly and sweet chestnut. When the path divides take the left-hand path and keep on over all crosstracks to a gate leading to the Woodgreen road. Cross straight over and go through the gate into Godshill Inclosure. Follow the path ahead and turn right down the first path on the right. (It is opposite a turning leading to two paths on the left.) This leads you to a gate opening out of the inclosure onto the hillside with Godshill across the valley. Here you have a choice of return routes. The shorter route follows the lane back to the village. Turn right from the inclosure gate to the metalled lane. Bear left, past a junction and continue to follow the lane as it dips over a stream crossed by a footbridge and climbs uphill back to the Fighting Cocks.

To take the longer route, turn left from the inclosure gate past a Forestry Commission barrier and follow the main path for a few yards as it curves right. To the left you will see two white paths. Ignore a green path on the right leading steeply downhill and follow the next path on the right (the first of the two white paths) which curves round the hillside, dividing then meeting again after a few yards. Below you will see a clear path leading over the valley. Follow the narrow track as it bears left then right to meet this wider path descending the hillside to a stream. The water is shallow and easy to cross but without wellies it may be necessary to paddle! Climb the lower part of the slope ahead and look for an iron gate on the right. Turn right through the gate and follow the hillside path with the fence on your right. A wide track leads you back to the Woodgreen road. Turn right to walk up to the pub.

⑮ North Gorley
The Royal Oak

North Gorley is a small village of old world cottages, clustered around wide greens where ponies, sheep and cattle can still be pastured. The villagers' ducks and geese keep cool in a tree-shaded pond. As this tiny settlement is just outside the western boundary of the Forest these ancient rights of common were not extinguished under Forest law in 1079 and as you drive into the village you may feel that very little has changed since then! Overlooking the pond stands the 17th century pub, the Royal Oak, low-thatched and white-walled.

Families are very welcome at the Royal Oak. Inside there is a multi-purpose function and family room and outside a special play area for children. Meals are served 12-2 and 6.30-9.30 Monday to Saturday and on Sunday from 12-2 and 7-9.30. On the menu you will find an interesting and varied range of home-made dishes including fresh fish as well as the traditional ploughman's and 'doorstep toasties' with delicious fillings. Children have their own menu. Drinking hours

70

are from 11-2.30 and 6-11 Monday to Friday, 11-3 and 6-11 on Saturday and normal hours on Sunday. Several real ales are available and Inch's Stonehouse cider is on tap.

Dogs are welcome but it is wise to keep them on a lead. Walkers may leave cars but the landlord requests that patrons park sensibly.
Telephone: 01425 652244

How to get there: North Gorley is about 4 miles north of Ringwood. Follow the A338 from Ringwood in the direction of Fordingbridge. The turning for North Gorley is on the right. At the T-junction turn left and after a few yards bear a little left again to continue north to The Royal Oak which is on the left.

Parking: At the pub.

Length of the walk: 2 ¹/₂ miles. Map: OS Outdoor Leisure 22 New Forest

Variety is the keynote of this scenic walk. From a picturesque village in the Avon valley the walk climbs a ridge to enter the completely different world of the Forest with its rolling heaths and ancient woodlands. As you follow the ridge you have fine views of both worlds, and the many small homesteads that flourish in this border country.

The Walk
With the front of the pub on your right and the village pond on your left walk along the green beside the road and turn left up the lane signed for Hyde and Frogham. Forest trees shade the lane as it climbs gently uphill to divide in front of a grassy triangle. Turn right. The way soon becomes a gravel track, bears left and starts to climb more steeply. Just past a house on the left the track divides. The more obvious way bears left but ignore this and keep straight on uphill along a narrow path through the bracken. After a few yards you meet a good crosstrack. Turn right to follow this splendid ridge walk along the top of Gorley Hill. On the right the hill slopes down to the Avon valley with wide views of the river winding through the meadows like a silver ribbon. Looking south you will see Hengistbury Head against the horizon, and to the north the Wiltshire downs. East, across Gorley Common, lies the medieval landscape of the New

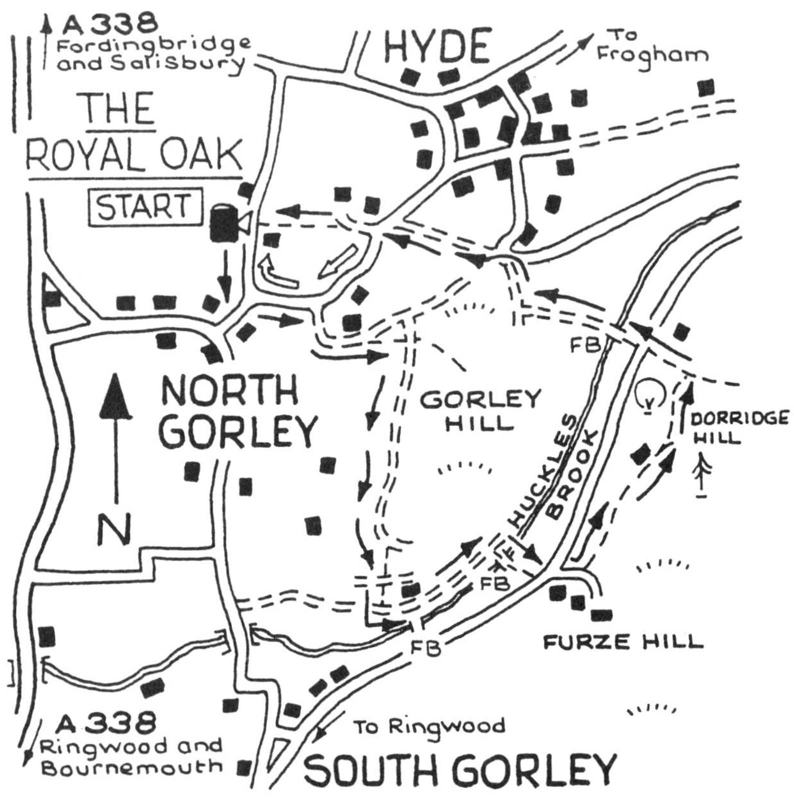

Forest. In the Forest, the Commoners' rights were carefully defined and limited. Some rights are staunchly maintained today and include the right of pasturage for ponies and cattle (after payment of a fee), the right to pasture pigs during the pannage season when there are plentiful supplies of acorns and beech mast, and the right to gather fuel and dig peat.

When the main path bears left keep straight on downhill with a small wood on your left. Go over a crosstrack and keep on over the track leading to a house, Gorley Firs. After a few yards you meet a gravel crosstrack. Turn left and follow this track as it curves round the foot of Gorley Hill and runs gently downhill between high hedges to reach the green lawns beside Huckles Brook. As the track turns a little left away from the stream you will see a small concrete bridge on the right. Ignore this bridge and continue past a track leading to a ford. (This is not the ford marked on the OS map which is further north.) Keep on along the gravel track which ends in front of a gate. Just to the right of the gate you will see a tiny bridge over a gully. Cross this and follow a narrow path which bears right to a well-made wooden footbridge over Huckles Brook. Cross and keep ahead (not the path along the streamside) to a minor road.

Walk over the road and go up the lane ahead — past a no-through-road sign — for about 60 yards. Over the grass on the left you will see a white path. Turn left to follow this path with a thicket of bushes on your right. The path becomes wider and gravelled and begins to climb uphill towards the oaks and beeches encircling Dorridge Hill. This is a splendid place for deer spotting.

At the approach to the wooded hill you pass a cattery (with obvious signs of once being a stables) on the left. Turn left just past the cattery to walk through the trees with rising ground on your right. The path bears left downhill to leave the wood and return to the minor road. Cross the road and continue into the valley to cross a footbridge over Huckles Brook. A good track leads ahead uphill past a turning on the right to a crosstrack. Bear right and keep on to meet another track. At this point you will see the corner of a minor road about 20 yards away on the right. Do not take the track immediately on the left but walk in the direction of the road for a few yards towards a high hedge on the left. Before the hedge, turn left and walk on over the grass keeping the hedge close on your right. When the hedge gives way to a high embankment continue as before keeping the embankment on your right. Go straight over a crosstrack to a minor road.

Turn left along the road for a few yards and now you have a choice of routes. On the right a lane leads to a grass track which can be very muddy but does run straight down to North Gorley to emerge out of the trees opposite the Royal Oak. If your footwear is up to it, turn right down the lane for a few yards to a gate. On the left of the gate the path continues steeply downhill past a footpath sign on the right, back to the village. Or, to avoid the mud, do not turn right down the lane, but keep on down the minor road to rejoin the route we followed from the village at the start of the walk by the grassy triangle. Follow the road as it bears right back to the village, turning right for The Royal Oak. If you enjoyed this walk you may like to read Heywood Sumner's delightful book *Cuckoo Hill* in which he describes his home in the village and the people he knew there.

Canada
The Rockingham Arms

Canada is a long village running along the edge of an area that was formerly common land on the north-east boundary of the Forest. But why the name Canada? It is believed that the small settlement was made originally by some would-be emigrants to Canada who for some reason decided to make the Forest their home instead. They chose wisely as the beautiful rolling heathland around the village offered good grazing for their animals as it still does today.

There is direct access to the Forest from the Rockingham Arms. This is a pub with something to suit everyone. Walkers with muddy boots can enjoy full meals or snacks in the cool stone-flagged bar and a splendid a la carte service is available in the restaurant. There is plenty of room inside for children and an enclosed play area for them in the garden. A charming feature of the garden is the old well. Meals are served from 12-2.30 and from 7-10 and during the week there is a special reduced rate for Senior Citizens. Most of the tempting food on offer is home-cooked and includes some interesting Canadian dishes. A range of delicious sauces (flavoured with whisky, pepper and mustard) is featured. The restaurant is very popular so coming as a large group it is wise to book beforehand.

Drinking hours are from 11.45-2.30 and 6-11 with normal hours on Sunday. A variety of real ales is available including London Pride and Theakstons. Draught cider is Dry Blackthorn and Red Rock. You can choose from an extensive wine list. Walkers are welcome to leave their cars in the large car park and there is no objection to dogs on leads.

Telephone: 01794 322473

How to get there: Canada is beside a minor road signed from the A36, the main road between Southampton and Salisbury. Look for the turning as the road runs through West Wellow. The pub is about ³/₄ mile down the minor road on the right.

Parking: Walkers may leave their cars in the pub car park.

Length of the walk: 2 ¹/₂ miles. Map: OS Outdoor Leisure 22 New Forest.

The open heaths of the Forest, the springy turf cropped short by grazing animals, offer wonderful walking with wide views. This walk crosses one of the most attractive of the Forest heaths and leads to Sturtmoor Pond, a remote stretch of water rich in wildlife. The heath attracts many birds including lapwings, stonechats and nightjars.

The Walk

With your back to the pub restaurant, cross the car park at the rear of the pub and climb the stiles to walk on over two paddocks. A stile beside a wooden door leads to a lane. The wide heath of West Wellow Common opens before you. Turn left to follow the lane with the common on your right. 'Wellow' is derived from a Celtic word meaning 'watery blue' which describes the small stream that runs through the parish. The parish is very old and is recorded in a document as early as 553AD. In his will made some years before his death in 901AD, King Alfred left Wellow to his daughter, the warrior princess Ethelfleda.

Follow the lane to a junction with a minor road on the left. Opposite, on your right, is a gravelled parking area at the approach

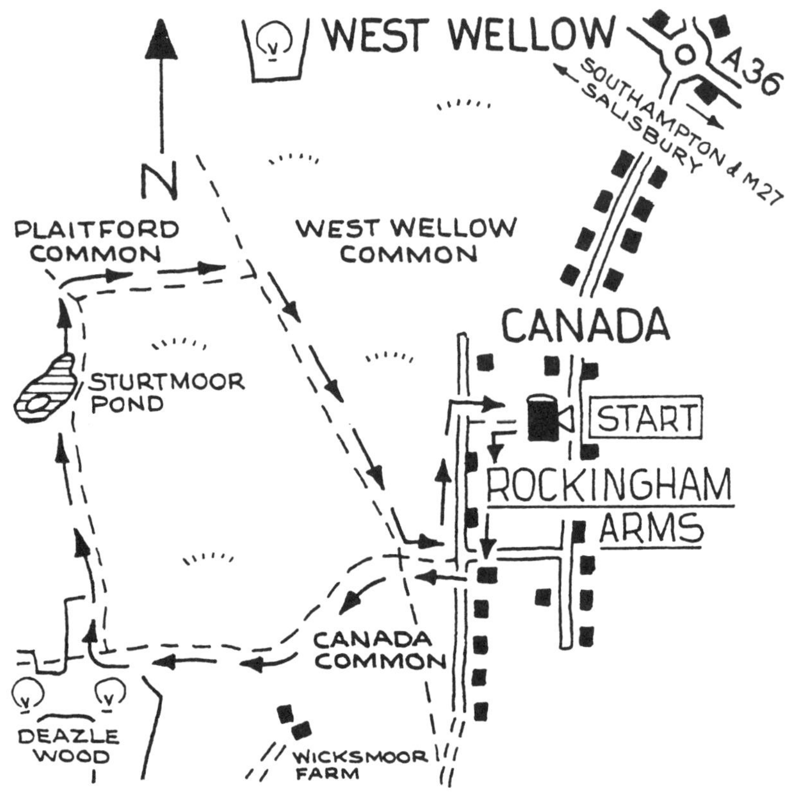

to Canada Common. Turn right over the gravel making for the far left-hand edge. At this point, the path is not well-defined, but keep ahead over the grassy area between the gorse bushes and after a few yards you will see a good path leading over the common towards a distant belt of woodland. Take this path as it winds over the heath keeping the woodland always ahead. This is a medieval landscape where donkeys, cattle, ponies and the occasional pig roam freely over unfenced country.

Keep ahead over a crosstrack. The path on the right is the return route. After a few yards the path continues over Plaitford Common, the property of the National Trust and an SSSI. The common is noted for rare wetland plants and lichens. As you approach closer to the woods an outcrop of old trees reaches like a finger across your path. Do not continue into the wood but leave the main path and turn right

Lonely Sturtmoor pond provides a welcome drink for commoners' animals.

with the finger of woodland on your left. There is a narrow path to follow. When the trees give way to heath again bear right for just a few yards. Turn to resume your original heading with your back to the woods and ahead you will see a gleam of water. This is Sturtmoor Pond. Walk towards the pond soon picking up a good path which leads you to the right-hand bank. The pond is surrounded by green lawns and dotted with islands. Swifts dart and skim the surface and you may see a heron fishing in the nearby marshes.

From the right-hand bank, with the pond on your left, bear a little right to follow the path for a few yards uphill through the gorse bushes. Before leaving the bushes the path divides. Take the right-hand path which leads over the open heath in the direction of Canada. After climbing a slight rise you will see the houses of the village in the distance. The path leads to a crosstrack. Turn right to follow a rutted way to rejoin the path you followed over Canada Common earlier in the walk (the next crosstrack). Turn left to retrace your steps to the gravelled area. Turn left down the lane and the door and stile leading to the path to the pub are on your right.

⓱ Bank
The Oak Inn

Only a minute or two from the busy A35, this pub stands in a beautiful Forest glade surrounded by the venerable trees from which it takes its name. Built as a cider house over 300 years ago, it is a family-owned pub with low beamed ceilings and a genuine Forest atmosphere. In cold weather a log fire blazes in the fireplace. This is a most attractive feature surrounded by tiles depicting scenes from Shakespeare's plays. When nearby Cuffnells House was demolished the fireplace was rescued by the present landlord's father. Cuffnells was the home of Alice Hargreaves, the little girl who was the original Alice of *Alice in Wonderland*. Lewis Carroll was a frequent visitor to the house and must have admired the tiles!

Families are welcome at mealtimes and the woodland garden with its chipmunks and pigmy goats will appeal especially to children. All the food is home-cooked, including huge ham joints. After a walk you can choose from a menu which includes a proper old-fashioned stew, venison sausages and a variety of unusual soups including Stilton-and-watercress. There is a special menu for children. Meals are served every lunchtime from 12-2. Evening meals are served from 6.30-9.30 except on Sunday and Monday. As this Inn is very popular it is advisable for large groups to book beforehand.

Drinking hours are from 11.30-2.30 and 6-11 throughout the week with normal hours on Sunday. A range of real ales includes Tanglefoot, Woodhouse draught Bass and Ringwood Best. A tempting range of Gales country wines is on offer and Scrumpy Jack and Bulmers Original draught cider.

Dogs on leads are no problem and walkers are welcome to leave their cars.

Telephone: 01703 282350.

How to get there: Leave Lyndhurst on the A35 in the direction of Bournemouth. After about 3/4 mile turn left for Bank. The Oak Inn is a few yards down the lane on the right.

Parking: In the pub car park.

Length of the walk: 2 miles. Map: OS Outdoor Leisure 22 New Forest.

A thousand years of New Forest history comes alive during this short walk. The route visits a Saxon settlement, still remote and isolated in its Forest clearing and then passes one of the great Victorian houses whose inhabitants had so great an effect on village life in the past.

The Walk

With the front of the pub on your right, turn right down the lane. Each side is lined by attractive houses, some old and half-timbered, with pretty gardens. Follow the lane as it runs a little downhill and curves left past an 'Access to houses only' notice. A few yards further on turn right down the next lane which runs past a house. The metalling finishes here. Keep ahead along a green footpath through the trees. The path bears right and becomes a track which leads past a house to meet a narrow lane. Turn left along the lane which heads west through the fine oaks and beeches of Gritnam Wood, one of the most beautiful old woods in the Forest. In the past, many more people made their living in the woods. You might have met charcoal burners, gypsies, swineherds and snake-catchers. The most famous

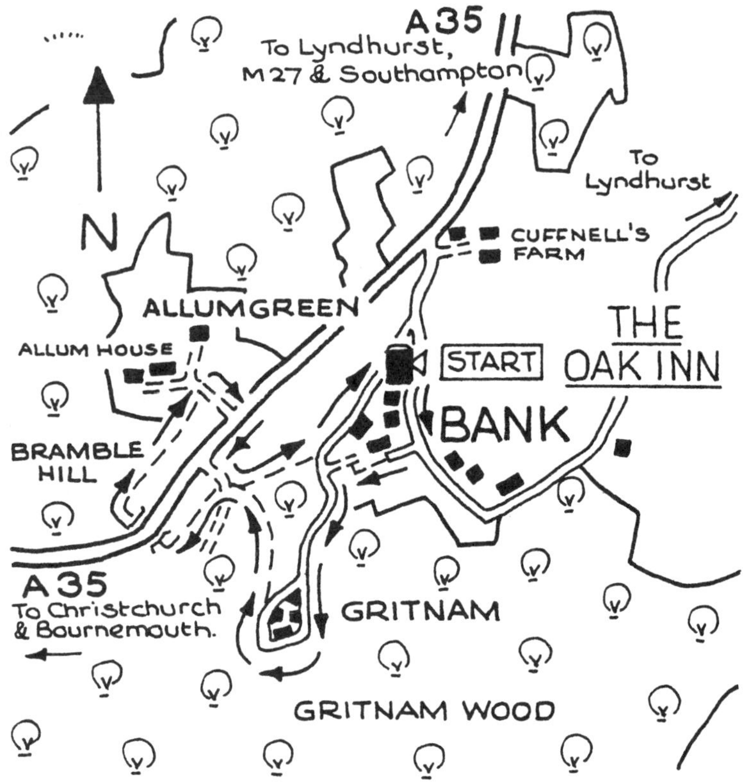

snake-catcher, Brusher Mills, lived in a wigwam-shaped hut of branches and turf in Gritnam Wood. Snake fat was much valued for medicinal purposes. Brusher Mills became well-known at Brockenhurst where he entertained passing coach travellers with his snakes. He is buried in the churchyard at Brockenhurst.

Soon you will see the cottages of Gritnam through the trees and as you enter the Forest clearing you will see the round hedge and fence that completely encircles this tiny hamlet. It is easy to imagine this as it would have been in Saxon times, a high pallisade protecting the inhabitants from the wolves and boars that once roamed the Forest. According to legend, the cottagers of Gritnam were once offered the opportunity to expand into the Forest by a grateful queen whose dress they had mended, but they preferred to stay as they were, tucked safely within their fence.

Allum House, built by the Fenwick family.

When the lane divides take the left-hand lane and follow it as it curves round the hamlet which is on your right. The lane drops downhill and begins to curve right to rejoin the lane by which you approached the village. Do not follow the lane right but on the corner turn left along a slightly gravelled path with your back to Gritnam. Follow the path straight ahead through the trees and over a cleared area. The path is faint at this point but bear a little left and you will see the path clearly again leading down to a gravelled track. Follow the gravelled track towards a gate opening onto the A35. Just before the gate turn left over the grass to follow a woodland path parallel with the A35 which is through the trees on your right. When the path divides, turn right along the gully running under the A35. Walk up the gully ahead to within a few yards of the point where it begins to flatten, and turn right up the bank. You will see a woodland path ahead. Follow this with the A35 now 100 yards or so away behind the trees on your right.

Soon you will see the stables of Allum House ahead. Bear right to look back at Allum House, beautifully framed by Forest trees. This fine house is typical of many family homes built by wealthy business or professional men after the coming of the railway in the mid 19th century had made the Forest more accessible. The Forest provided the seclusion and sporting facilities such homes required without the need to maintain an estate. It was once the home of the Fenwick family who donated the hospital, which bears their name, to Lyndhurst in 1908.

Follow the gravel track to the A35, cross the road and turn right to walk a few yards along the roadside to a gate on the left. Go through the gate or climb the stile beside it to return to the gravel track followed earlier from Gritnam. Follow the gravel track to the point where it turns right. Keep straight on here, still retracing your steps, over the grass for about 100 yards to the open area. The route to Gritnam leads over the grass ahead, bearing a little right. Do not take this but cross the grass bearing slightly left towards a post supporting power lines. After a few yards the path is clear and leads to the left of the post towards a house in Bank which you will see through the trees ahead. In front of the house you meet a lane. Keep ahead up the lane which leads past Annesley House. The Victorian novelist Mary Braddon wrote *Lady Audley's Secret* here. The book caused a sensation and sold over a million copies. Follow the lane a few yards further to the Oak Inn which is on your right.

⓲ Blackfield
The Bridge Tavern

East of the Beaulieu river, the Dark Water flows to the Solent through a beautiful remote valley. The Bridge Tavern is the ideal gateway to this little-known area. In one of the most attractive areas of the valley beside a streamside garden, the tavern is a traditional Forest pub, with a cosy, welcoming atmosphere. Special facilities are provided for wheelchairs. Meals are served from 12-2.30 (in winter until 2) and in the evening from 6.30-9.30 (Sunday 7-9). One glance at the menu and the array of tempting dishes on the specials board should reassure the hungriest of walkers! Homemade steak and kidney pies and puddings and creamy-topped lasagne are always popular. From the specials board we were tempted by poached salmon in dill and vegetable crostini followed by rum log and cream. There is also a varied menu for children. Such good food makes the tavern deservedly busy so it is advisable to book.

Drinking hours in summer are from 11-3 (Sunday 12-3) and from 5.30-11 (Sunday 7-10.30). In winter from 12-2.30 and from 6-11 (Sunday 7-10.30). Real ales are Wadworth 6X, Speckled Hen and Ringwood Best Bitter. The house cider is Strongbow and there is a wide selection of wines which are available by the glass. All this can be enjoyed in cold weather before a blazing log fire. In summer you may prefer to sit outside on the patio which overlooks the children's play area and has lovely views down the Dark Water valley to King's Copse.

Dogs on leads are welcome in the public bar and no one objects to patrons leaving their cars in the car park while they walk.

Telephone: 01703 892554.

How to get there: Take the A326 in the direction of Fawley. Continue down the Waterside through Hardley and just before the junction with the B3053 (Calshot road) in Fawley turn right in the direction of Beaulieu. Follow signs for Beaulieu for 2 miles. The road dips to a bridge over the Dark Water and The Bridge Tavern is on the left.

Parking: In the pub car park.

Length of the walk: 3 miles. Map: OS Outdoor Leisure 22 New Forest.

This is an easy walk in a less often visited part of the Forest. Surprisingly, Fawley is only 2 miles away over the heath but as you explore the peaceful Dark Water valley it could be on another planet! The varied scenery includes heath and woodland and an ancient trackway, possibly made by Celtic tribes before the coming of the Romans.

The Walk

Leave the front of the pub on your right and walk up the road. After a few yards there is a narrow footpath beside the road. If you look down over the shallow green meadows beside the Dark Water on your left you will see they are ridged and embanked and there appears to be the remains of a moat. In medieval days Holbury Manor owned by the monks of Beaulieu, stood here. 'Holbury' means 'a fortress in a hollow' and the settlement in the valley can be traced back to Roman times.

At the top of the hill, opposite Park Lane, turn right to follow a good track signed as a bridleway. This pleasant way runs towards the iron gates of Green Rollestone House. In front of the gates the track turns left. Trees shade the attractive path ahead as it follows the edge of meadows on the left and thicker woodland on the right. Where

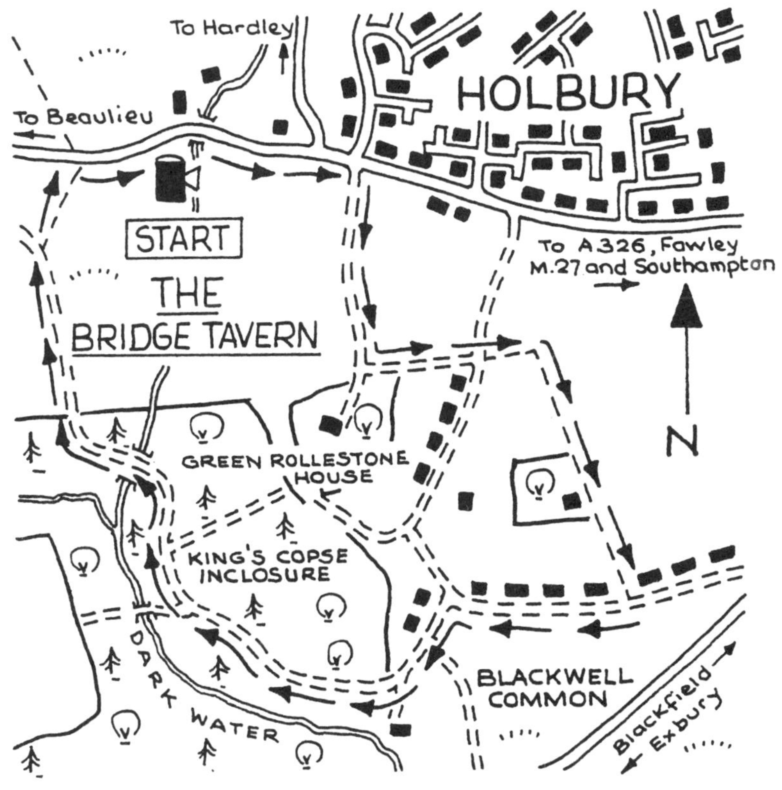

woods and cultivated land meet, wild flowers seem to flourish and this is a marvellous place for bluebells. Go through a gate and keep straight on over a crosstrack. Ahead lies a completely different path, a wide greenway which I believe could be the route of an ancient British track. As you follow it you will see it is very flat and raised and almost all grassed over. Unlike most woodland ways it is straight and determined in direction. A known British track can be traced in Fawley Inclosure and as this would run quite close to the Dark Water on its way to the port at Lepe, it seems likely that this greenway formed part of the route. Among other commodities, Cornish tin was traded long before the Romans built their roads in the first four centuries AD.

The greenway bears right and continues to meet a lane. Open heathland stretches ahead and on the horizon are the blue shadows

The Dark Water.

of the Isle of Wight hills. Turn right to walk over the heath beside the lane with houses on your right. The line of houses gives way to heath and the lane divides before a crosstrack. Take the left-hand track and keep to this main track as it curves round two houses on the right. As you approach the wooded valley of the Dark Water the track divides. One track leads past a Forestry Commission barrier towards a small Forest homestead. Do not take this one, but follow the other track as it curves right and runs downhill through a gate into King's Copse Inclosure, the peaceful woods beside the Dark Water. Forest scenes surround you and the only sounds I heard when I came this way were the sighing of the wind in the trees and the crowing of the homestead cock. These must have been familiar sounds to the men of the New Stone Age, the first farmers, who settled this valley over four thousand years ago. Three hundred of their flint tools have been found.

Follow the main track, ignoring all side tracks, as it slowly descends into the valley. When the track forms a Y-junction, take the right-hand track (the left-hand track leads to a footbridge) which climbs to another junction. Bear left with the hillside descending to the Dark Water on your left. The track bends left to lead down to a small bridge over the Dark Water. This tiny stream in its quiet setting was a favourite haunt of the author and naturalist WH Hudson. Today it is still as he describes it in his fine book, *Hampshire Days*. 'I sought and found the stream well named the Dark Water' he writes, 'but when the sunlight falls on it the water is the colour of old sherry from the red soil it flows over.'

Continue up the track as it climbs the other side of the valley and goes through a gate to leave the inclosure. Keep straight on over the car parking area to the heath ahead. A prominent gravel track leads over the heath but do not follow this. Instead take the heathland path to the right of the gravel track which at first runs in the same direction. This gradually bears right and divides. Take the right-hand path and follow this to the road. Turn right to walk back to the Bridge Tavern.

19 **Linwood**
The Red Shoot Inn

Some of the loveliest scenery in the Forest surrounds this attractive inn. It overlooks the old oaks and beeches of Red Shoot Wood from which it takes its name and to the north and west it is sheltered by heather-covered hills. Once it was the village store and post office — the present landlord recalls seeing petrol pumps outside — and although considerably enlarged it still retains a comfortable old world atmosphere. I was impressed by the huge family room and the special facilities for the disabled.

Meals are served every lunchtime from 12-2 and in the evenings from 6.30-9 Monday to Thursday. Friday and Saturday from 6.30-10, and Sunday from 6.30-9. Summer weekends breakfast is available from 9-10.30. As well as daily specials from the blackboard there is a wide selection of main dishes including the inn's speciality Red Shoot Sizzling Steaks. Fish fillets come deep fried in beer batter and there is also a range of Light Bites and interesting sandwiches including ham-and-pineapple and Stilton-and-walnut. For Senior Citizens there is a reduced price menu and a menu for children.

Drinking hours are from 11-11 in summer and from 11-3 and 6-11 in winter. Real ales include Wadworth 6X, Henry's PA, Farmers Glory and Ringwood Best. Draught ciders are Dry Blackthorn and Woodpeckers. There is an extensive wine list or you can purchase house wines by the glass. Beside the pub is an inviting beer garden shaded by Forest trees. No one objects to walkers leaving their cars and, as the notice outside says 'Muddy boots, dogs and well-behaved owners welcome'!
Telephone: 01425 475792

How to get there: Approaching from the west, take the turning for Lyndhurst off the A338 about 2 ½ miles north of Ringwood. The pub is on the left, set back from the road, after about 3 miles. Approaching from Lyndhurst, take the A35 (Bournemouth) road, turn right just past the village for Emery Down. Pass the New Forest Inn take the Bolderwood road and continue, to drive under the A31. The road bears left for Linwood and the pub is on your right after 3 ½ miles.

Parking: In the pub car park.

Length of the walk: 2 ½ miles. Map: OS Outdoor Leisure 22 New Forest.

All that is most appealing about the New Forest can be seen on this walk: wide heathland views, tiny streams with pebble beaches, magnificent oak and beech woodland and some of its rich wildlife, including — if you are lucky — roe and fallow deer.

The Walk
With the front of the pub on your left follow the narrow lane that leads to the road. Walk along the grass beside the road under the trees for about 100 yards to a gravelled track on the left. Turn left to follow this past an attractive thatched cottage. Cross a cattle grid and now the path bears a little left then right to run between a high bank covered in wild flowers and meadows framed by sloping heathland. When the track curves right to a farm, keep straight on down a grassy track towards a gate. Cross the stile to the left of the gate. Do not be too perturbed by the sign about adders. Do take care, but bear in mind that they are more afraid of you than you are of them and will quickly get out of your way when they hear you coming. Cross the

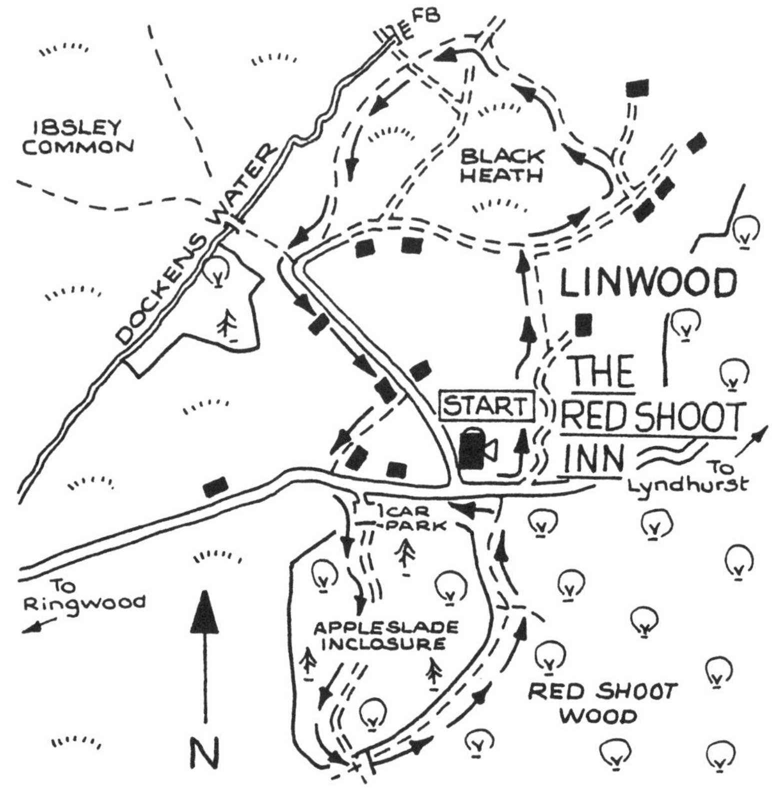

field ahead with the hedge on your right and go through the gate to meet a gravelled track. Suddenly the farming world vanishes and the undulating moorland of Black Heath opens before you.

Turn right to follow the track beside the heath. In front of a cottage the track curves left and climbs a little to give wide moorland views. Rising to the west are the slopes of Ibsley Common. When the track turns right to a house, bear left past a Forestry Commission barrier to follow the path over the heath. The path turns a little left to follow a moorland ridge and reveal a splendid view over the valley of Dockens Water on the right before running downhill past a Forestry Commission barrier. At this point you meet a gravel crosstrack. The route does turn left but do not take the gravel track as there is a prettier path beside Dockens Water. Cross straight over the track and continue for a few yards over the grass towards a fence.

Turn left along a narrow path with the fence on your right. This becomes a wide path which follows the bank of Dockens Water, one of the Forest's loveliest streams. There is a particularly delightful place where the stream has carved a deep channel and runs under a footbridge.

Continue along the path as it leaves the streamside to bear left and bring you to a lane. Turn right along the lane which turns left uphill. Climb the hill and just after a white house on the right, opposite a farm entrance, look carefully for a footpath sign beside a gate on the right. Turn right to walk along the top of a field with a hedge on your right. Cross the stile and go through a small wooden gate to a gravel track. This runs close to a house, but it is a right-of-way. Follow the gravel track through a gate to the road beside a footpath sign.

Turn left for a few yards, then bear right to cross the road to the entrance to Appleslade car park. Walk over the parking area and keep straight on through the gate ahead following the main track into the inclosure. Keep to the main track through these old woods, ignoring all side tracks. The track rises and runs past some gateposts to a clear area where there are several paths. Turn left along a wide grassy path which runs close to a low embankment marking an inclosure boundary on the left. This embankment is now your guide for all but the last few yards of the return route. Look for deer along this quiet woodland path. The Forest is home to fallow, roe, red, sika and muntjac. Only a few of the great herds of red deer that once roamed the Forest remain as nowadays there is probably not enough cover for them. Sika and muntjac favour the southern Forest so you are most likely to see fallow, the bucks recognisable by their wide spreading antlers, or roe who look like adverts for Babycham with small upright antlers. Follow the path beside the embankment over a crosspath and keep to the path as it bears left downhill. The path now leaves the embankment to cross the grass ahead to the road. Turn left to walk the few yards back to the Red Shoot Inn.

20 Burley
The Queen's Head

Cradled in the moors and protected to the west by a high ridge crowned with an Iron Age hill fort, Burley is a true Forest village. Once a tiny settlement clustered around its manor, depending for its livelihood on its yearly crop of acorns and beechmast, it has grown as Forest villages do, in a relaxed fashion to form several small communities. Today the narrow main street leading downhill from the crossroads by the war memorial is well-known for its craft shops and is often thronged with visitors. But a few steps away you will find remote Forest woods and heaths where it is easy to recapture Burley's colourful past.

The best place to start is Burley's old smuggling pub, the Queen's Head. Most of the paths leading from the pub into the Forest are smugglers' tracks and records dating back to 1633 tell of smugglers' horses buried under the floor and a secret tunnel to Burley Manor. Recently a smugglers' cellar with pistols, bottles and old coins was discovered under one of the bars. Conversation today is more likely to be centred around the excellent menu than the price of smuggled

French brandy and tobacco. A splendid choice is on offer including an assortment of pies and Viking Gammon – ham with a cheese and tomato topping. Another delicious dish is double-breasted chicken topped with lemon and black pepper. From the sweets board I was tempted by a chocolate sponge drenched in rum and topped with chocolate chips and truffles. The pub is large with plenty of room for families and meals are served from midday to 9 in the evening. On Sunday the bar closes at 3. Apart from normal Sunday opening, drinks are available every day from 11-11. Real ales include Flowers Original, London Pride, and Boddington's Bitter. Strongbow cider is on tap and the wine list is supplemented by an assortment of delicious country wines.

There is satellite television, a play area for children in the garden and in summer you can take wagonette rides from the pub forecourt. Dogs are welcome in the garden.

Telephone: 01425 403423

How to get there: From Lyndhurst take the A35 (Bournemouth) road. After about 6 miles turn right (Station Road) for Burley. In a little more than 2 miles the road drops to the crossroads in the village. The Queen's Head is immediately opposite.

Parking: In the pub car park or, if this is full, the adjacent public car park.

Length of the walk: 3 miles. Map: OS Outdoor Leisure 22 New Forest.

From the pub, an easy climb brings you to Burley Hill Fort, with its magnificent views over the western Forest and the Avon valley. So this is a perfect walk for a sunny summer evening as you can watch the sun set behind the distant outline of the Wiltshire downs. The return route follows green paths through ancient oak and beech woods.

The Walk

With your back to the front of the pub, turn right, then bear right again with the war memorial on your left, to walk down Burley's main street, the Ringwood Road. Pass the entrance to Burley Manor, now a hotel. Follow the footpath beside the road to leave the village behind and walk beside high hedges shaded by Forest oaks. Continue

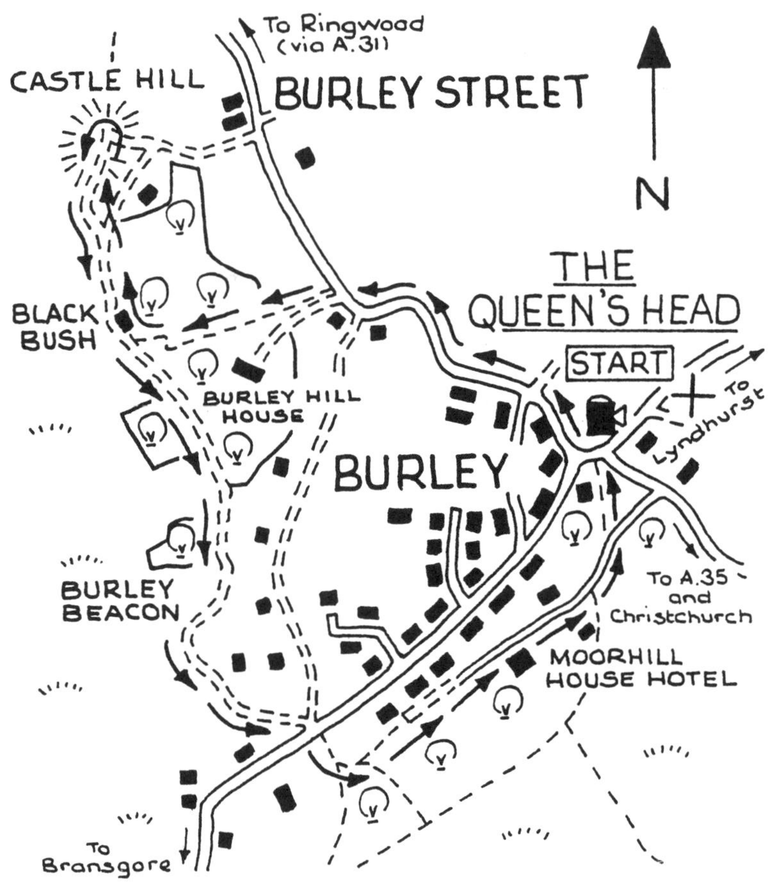

to the entrance of Clough Lane, then cross the road and take the raised footpath signed Burley Street. There are pleasant views over meadows and small woods on your right. When the path drops down to the road again, cross over and continue along the pavement for just a few yards to the wide entrance leading to a set of iron gates barring the drive to Burley Hill House. A right-of-way leads through the smaller right-hand gate. (An inconspicuous footpath sign indicates the way.) Turn left to go through the gate and follow the fenced footpath ahead.

The path winds gently uphill to enter a wood and cross streams by small rustic bridges. As you climb the hill surrounded by a tangle

94

Wagonette rides can be taken from the Queen's Head.

of old trees shading carpets of bluebells in spring, you may see roe deer. Cross the stile at the top of the hill to emerge on the high ridge west of Burley. The view is partly obscured by trees at this point but already there are glimpses over the spreading moorlands beneath the hillside. Turn right to follow the track through the trees past Black Bush cottages. When the track begins to rise and the trees give way to open grassy slopes on the left you have reached the hill fort. Turn left to follow one of the defensive embankments to enjoy a wonderful view. Looking south-west you can see as far as Old Harry and the Purbeck Hills. Directly beneath the fort the ridged outline of a smugglers' path snakes north over Vales Moor to Picket Post. The minor road leading west is an old Saxon war path. 'Burley' means 'a fortified place in a clearing'. It seems that the whole area was the scene of many conflicts which are commemorated in such place names as 'Burnt Axon' and 'Coffin Holms'.

Turn right from the fort to retrace your steps along the ridge, keep on the track ignoring the stile into the wood on the left. On the right you pass a flat grassy area shaded by well-spaced oaks, the site of Burley Beacon to be lit in times of danger, and the scene of the strangest battle of all. According to a document preserved in

Berkeley Castle, on this spot the brave Sir Morris Barkley assisted by his two dogs, slew 'a devouring dragon'. This seems rather a pity as the dragon was evidently a mild-mannered creature only requiring a pail of milk occasionally!

Continue past a track on the left and follow the track as it descends the hill and curves left to meet a road. Cross straight over and take the footpath ahead which becomes a wide greenway leading into old oak, beech and rowan woods. Shortly the path divides. Follow the main path left with a fence on your left. The fence running along the top of a low embankment is now your guide. The path climbs a little uphill and divides. Take the left-hand path, keeping the fence a few yards away on your left. Just past a house on the other side of the fence the path runs past a Forestry Commission barrier. Continue along the track ahead past the next house with a hedge on your left to more houses where the track becomes a metalled lane. Pass the Moorhill House Hotel and now the lane runs downhill to follow a valley with attractive cottages and gardens. The lane climbs through woods to a gravelled car park beside Station Road. Do not go to the road but keep straight on past the house sign for Brenchley to a Forestry Commission barrier. From the barrier ignore the more obvious track leading ahead and bear a little to the left of it through the trees. After a few yards the path becomes more clearly defined and drops steeply past some wooden fencing to the road opposite the Queen's Head.